Crazyman's Economics

T.E. Scott
As Told To Stephen Edds

First published by Dog Ear Publishing
4010 W. 86th Street, Ste H
Indianapolis, IN 46268
www.dogearpublishing.net

ISBN: 978-159858-640-4
Library of Congress Control Number: Applied for

This book is printed on acid-free paper.

Printed in the United States of America

— About the authors —

T.E. Scott spent 32 years working for Eastern Airlines and lost a majority of his pension when the company went bankrupt in the 1980s. He and his late wife started a business selling dog leads and collars out of their home, and built it into Scott Pet Products, a multi-million dollar company in Rockville, Indiana. Scott retired and has spend the last several years developing the ideas and concepts for this book. Scott lives at the "Crazyman's Hideaway" in Veedersburg, Indiana.

CrazymansEconomics.com

Stephen Edds is a native of Owensboro, Kentucky and is a graduate of Hanover (IN) College. Edds spent 15 years in corporate marketing communications before striking out on his own as a freelance writer. Edds moved to Indianapolis, IN, in 1996, and currently resides there with his wife, Erin, and son Levi.

stephenedds.com

— Contents —

— Foreword —

You should be outraged.
You should know better.
You should be storming the Capitol demanding reform.
But you're not outraged.
And you don't know better.
Neither did I, until recently.

When I met T.E. Scott, I was (and am) struggling as a freelance writer, working in a nightmare corporate job and looking for a way out. So, when the opportunity was presented to write a book on the stock market, I jumped at the chance.

When T.E. explained the premise of the book, my initial reaction to my role as a co-author would be similar to that of a defense attorney. I didn't necessarily need to understand or believe my client—I just needed to present the best case for him.

Over the course of several months, I made multiple trips to Veedersburg, Indiana, to capture his thoughts on paper. We had vigorous debates, where I challenged his beliefs and he challenged mine. Meanwhile, I began to research the markets to see if I could find any corresponding evidence. Then it sank in...he's onto something.

I bombarded T.E. with articles, books, news reports to lend credibility to his ideas. I believed that once people read the facts, they would better understand his argument. TE didn't want that, though. He didn't want to clutter his message. He kept telling me, "You want to write a dang story for everything. We have got to keep it simple."

"Crazyman's Economics" is T.E. Scott's straightforward view of our conditioning to play a losing game when we start trusting in the markets. Based on his experiences, thoughts and observations, this book is direct, brief and to the point, not muddled up with a bunch of confusing facts and figures.

Those of you expecting a PhD-level academic explanation of how the markets work won't find it here. We're not investment advisors, so what you do with your money is up to you. Those of you looking for a way to "beat the system" won't find it here either. (Here's a hint: You can't.)

The main emphasis of the book is on getting you to rethink a concept you've accepted without question your entire life. We want the losers in the markets to quit losing and demand accountability from those in charge of managing your money. It's a formidable task to be sure, but the alternative is far worse.

Revolutions are not started by those in power. Revolutions begin with someone who has had enough, who has nothing left to lose. In T.E. Scott's case, it took losing his pension and starting over from scratch to make a self-made, barely educated man in west central Indiana question the very foundation of the American economy and figure out that it is a losing game to all but a very few.

T.E. has nothing to lose. You, on the other hand, have your retirement and pension to lose. You have the power to decide if the system we support should remain in place. If you are outraged, then together we can make our voices heard, demanding real accountability and bringing a corrupt system to its knees.

Sometimes, it takes a crazy man to change the system for the better.

Stephen Edds
March 2008

— Introduction —

My name is T.E. Scott, and this book was written to expose the stock market and commodity markets as the largest ongoing con games in United States history. I was a victim of this con as an employee at Eastern Airlines. I worked as a baggage handler for 32 years and was given "preferred stock" as part of my pay package. Funny thing is, when they went bankrupt, it must have been "preferred," they took it first.

I was lucky, I worked hard and started my own business in my living room and through sheer determination was able to build that into a successful privately owned company in west central Indiana. But I never forgot what guys like Frank Lorenzo at Eastern Airlines did to me and thousands of my co-workers. And I kept seeing it happening to average people every day, not only at Enron and World Com, but to the people I talked to in the diners in Veedersburg, Indiana where I live. People were getting ripped off in the markets and had no voice or recourse, and amazingly enough, some even thought it was their own fault.

I began thinking about the true nature of investments and how they're presented to us as opposed to what they really are. It should be a good deal only when all parties benefit. And yet, when you take a close look at the markets, there are no circumstances when all parties benefit. I also figured out that in a fair investment situation, five-percent net is a reasonable return on a cash investment.

To the left, you'll see a clover. You'll also see one on my overalls that I wear daily. This is a reminder that, when I want to run a company or judge how a company operates, I follow the 5 G's that I developed.

When I first started out, I had no reference point to judge a company. I developed the 5 G's as a measuring tool. If you see a company failing to follow one of the 5 G's, then someone is getting the short end of the stick. And when you apply the 5 G's to the markets, then who is it really good for?

People make fortunes in the markets, and that money has to come from some-where. Or more specifically, someone. Who is losing the money that all the people are winning? No one was asking that question, and I felt like someone needed to.

The last four years I've been thinking, talking, listening, and debating people about the function of the stock markets and commodities markets. I've studied how investments should work and how the markets actually work and have come to the unmistakable conclusion that the average American is getting fleeced and pillaged every day. It's time to fight back!

We have been conned for decades by a group I call the "Masters of Illusion and Deception." To keep it simple, I will refer to them throughout the book as the MASTERS.

There is no club, no roll call, and no meeting of this group. Who specifically is part of the MASTERS isn't the point.

These MASTERS are brilliant, greedy, powerful, influential, and addicted to wealth without remorse. Some may be evil, some may be greedy, and some may be blissfully ignorant of the con.

I wonder if they initially were motivated to seek wealth to accumulate power, or did they seek power to accumulate wealth? Maybe they're intertwined, but the one thing I'm certain of is they have targeted you as their prey.

You have been conned by the MASTERS. To fully understand how and why this has happened, one of the hardest things you'll have to do is ignore the information, advice, and the conditioning that you've accepted without question. Don't believe that the markets are ever working in your best interest.

"Crazyman's Economics" will simplify a very complex system that the MASTERS have designed, developed, and perfected over time to separate the masses from their money without accountability or prosecution. As a result of this design, they have tricked us into believing that the stock market and commodity markets are something they are not.

One way the MASTERS did this while avoiding scrutiny was to make the system so complex that no one fully understands it. To keep from getting tangled in their web of confusion and keep this simple, we are going to focus on the basics of the markets. This will prevent everyone from getting distracted by excess language that merely adds confusion to any understanding of the markets. There are no sections

Masters of Illusion and Deception (MASTERS) – A group that designed, developed, and keep the con in place. These MASTERS are brilliant, greedy, powerful, influential, and addicted to wealth without remorse.

Crazyman $ays:
"Don't believe what you have been conditioned to think, have been told or taught. Follow your $. Do your math. Facts are facts."

Minus-sum game –
Players as a whole in the
markets wind up at the
end of the day with less
$ than they started with.

addressing options, hedge funds,
indexing, selling short or long, because
the results are the same—it's all a con.

Plus, no matter how complicated they
make it, the basics are still the
same...you are participating in a minus-
sum game. I could write a 1,000-page
book about the complexities of the
system, and you would no more or less
understand what's happening then than
you do now.

Now, how did a high-school educated,
common man like me figure all this out?
Through my work, I began to see
through the illusions and deceptions
used to distract us and to ask simple
questions:

Here are some questions everyone
should ask when considering
participating in the markets:
- ▶ Where does the money come from
  when an investor wins?
- ▶ Where does the money go when an
  investor loses his or her money?
- ▶ Why aren't any financial records kept
  tracking investors' money?
- ▶ Why are brokers and money
  managers not required to produce
  records of how much money their
  clients lost?
- ▶ Why isn't the industry as a whole
  required to provide full disclosure
  and accountability of investors'
  money?
- ▶ Who actually controls the stock
  market and commodities markets?
- ▶ Why doesn't anyone question the
  real role of the regulatory
  commissions?

By asking these questions, and actively seeking answers, I figured out the MASTERS had hidden the truth of their motives, while covering themselves in countless disclaimers.

Like magicians, these MASTERS who control the markets create a spectacular show to distract you from the simple sleight-of-hand they are performing. No magician truthfully says they can saw a woman in half and then put her back together again. But you want to believe they can. The magicians do it for entertainment; the MASTERS do it to separate you from your money.

I'm going to make a startling claim throughout this book: **95 percent of investors lose money in the stock markets and commodity markets.** This number can be argued, debated, or ignored, but it cannot be disproved. I drew my own conclusions based on my evaluation of the system, but I do know for sure that the markets are a minus-sum game for average investors. More than 50 percent lose money just because of the way the markets are designed. If you consider in the added advantages that the select few Fat Cats enjoy, and factor in the number of companies that leave investors holding the bag when the shares are removed from trading, the percentages increase significantly.

I will point out throughout the book that no one can prove me wrong because the exchanges and brokers do not keep these records. The government does not require them, the media doesn't ask for them, the brokers and exchanges don't keep them, and investors take the

Players – Refers to all investors, traders, hedgers, speculators, clients, and other participants in the stock markets and commodity markets.

$ – I use the $ symbol to replace the term "money" to consistently remind you to focus on what the MASTERS and Fat Cats are focused on…your $.

Crazyman $ays:
"Motion takes $ out of the
pockets of players (-$) and
puts $ in the pockets
of Fat Cats."

brokers at their word without question. Until they can prove me wrong by showing a full accounting of total investors as a whole, instead of a hand-picked few, my 95 percent claim will stand.

Throughout the book, I will use terms and symbols to replace common words or phrases. It may appear as a gimmick at first, but these symbols ($, -$, *players*, MASTERS, etc.) are designed to help you rethink what you've been taught to believe and to focus on the arguments I'm presenting.

Early on, I figured out investors are simply *players* in the games the MASTERS developed. Therefore, I will replace all references to the terms investors, traders, hedgers, speculators and clients with "*players*." If you have money in the markets, you are a *player*, pure and simple. Those people who benefit from the illusions and deceptions and work them to their advantage are whom I refer to as Fat Cats. It's an almost comical term, but have no doubt, they are parasites who survive off of your money.

Look at all *players* as a whole to get a complete view of the markets. Looking at the success of a few people in the markets is playing into the hands of the MASTERS. You would not look at the winner of the lottery jackpot as a representative of all lottery participants as a whole, nor should you with *players* in the market. It's all about getting their hands on your money ($).

The MASTERS have you believing the illusion that you will make $ by playing the markets, and that the success of the markets is vital to the success of the economy. The deception is that those involved in your investments are working strictly in the best interest of you as a *player*. They've convinced you that participating in the market is a sound financial strategy vital to a strong economy. This is a lie.

Here's the fact: The total existence of the markets revolves around constantly changing prices and selling by the second to create motion. This motion takes $ out of the pockets of *players* (-$) and puts it in the pockets of Fat Cats. If all *players* play long enough, they will lose $ in time.

Crazyman $ays:
"If all things were equal,
all players would lose $
in time."

I can't stress enough that motion is the primary goal of everyone involved in your financial planning. This process keeps the markets functioning because it takes real cash from your pockets and replaces it with a piece of paper with published value, which is worthless unless you find someone else to buy it. Either way, they still have your $.

Despite all of the books, newsletters, analysts, and seminars that tell you how to beat the system, if all things were equal, all *players* will lose $ in time. My goal with "Crazyman's Economics" is simply to get the losers in the markets to quit losing. It's impossible for *players* as a whole to beat the markets. The only way to get the losers to quit losing is to quit participating. The great thing about this is that the losers are in control. This is one area in which we don't need our politicians to enact a federal law. If the losers in the markets quit losing, the lights will go out.

Eagle's Eye view – A tool used by the MASTERS, Fat Cats and brokers to avoid full disclosure. They focus your attention on what they want to promote, rather than providing real and complete statistics.

What I am presenting in **"Crazyman's Economics"** is not going to be popular to those who continue to profit by maintaining the status quo. They will attack me and attempt to discredit me by presenting anecdotal or incomplete information on individual successes to convince you that the system may not work for everyone, but it can work for you.

By exposing the illusions and deceptions the MASTERS used in designing their con game, I will show you some simple facts:

▶ The stock market and commodity markets are gambling facilities, no more and no less;

▶ The MASTERS are using weak words, the manipulation of statistics, lack of statistics, and psychological tricks in order to convince you that you are doing something other than gambling;

▶ Playing the markets is a minus-sum game, which means that at the end of the day, *players* wind up with less $ than they started with;

▶ Published value, perceived value, and outperformed are terms of illusion and deception;

▶ Brokers and money managers are not working in your best interests;

▶ You can't beat the system. If all things were equal, all *players* would lose $ in time.

I'm not going to allow you to be trapped in their web by letting them focus on the "Eagle's Eye view," which focuses on the success or failure of specific individuals. Instead I'm going to show you the formula of why the markets are a minus-sum game to *players* as a whole, and why you shouldn't be involved.

My critics will dismiss my simplistic approach as someone who "doesn't get it," and I will be rejected as a "conspiracy nut" in an effort to discredit me.

But the fact is there are countless books and articles addressing the flaws of the markets, without pointing out that the entire system itself is a con game. And, unlike most books, I have not devised a way to beat the system, because there isn't a way.

"Crazyman's Economics" will open your eyes to see that what you have been led to believe about the markets is a lie. You are part of an elaborate ongoing con game to separate you from your $. All I'm doing is exposing it as a gambling system for the average person to understand and hopefully avoid. I'm presenting a case that provides a straightforward explanation of a system that was designed to overwhelm us.

For real change to take place and for my message to get out, I'll need your help. Together, we can begin the process of empowering you to take charge of your investment and retirement by exposing the MASTERS and their elaborate con that slowly robs you of your $.

And when they can't win on facts, or provide honest, accurate statistics to prove their case, they'll dismiss me as being a "crazy man." In fact, I have to be somewhat crazy to take on the most brilliant and powerful con men in the world.

Chapter One:
— You can't beat the system —

Let's make this easy. There's no way to beat the system. From the moment you start playing by buying a share of stock or commodity contract, you are participating in a minus-sum game. At the end of the day, *players* (you) as a whole will lose $. That is not a theory, IT'S A FACT!

What am I talking about by a "minus-sum game?" *Players* are the only ones putting $ into the pot through buying shares of stock or commodity contracts. When a company sells a share, it takes $ out of the pot and does not give it back to the *players*. Brokers and the exchanges take a cut out of the *players'* pot every time *players* buy and sell thereafter. The company, brokers and exchanges are taking $ out of the pot, and *players* are the only ones putting $ in. *Players* as a whole will wind up with less $ in pocket at the end of the day than they started with. That should tell you right away that, if you're participating in a "minus-sum game," you can't beat the system.

Every day, people who put their hard-earned $ into commodity market contracts and shares in publicly traded companies in the stock market lose billions of dollars to the exchanges, brokerage firms, IRS, money managers, company shares, CEO stock options, and other *players*. The people who have designed the system are the Masters of Illusion and Deception (MASTERS), designed to separate the masses from their $ without accountability or prosecution. The rich and greedy that use this system to accumulate

Crazyman $ays:
*"Good information given
to too many people
becomes bad information."*

Minus-sum game –
Players as a whole in the
markets wind up at the
end of the day with less
$ than they started with.

wealth and power without remorse are the Fat Cats. The rest of us, the victims of their con games, are merely *players.* Now, you as a *player* believe you are investing when, in fact, you are playing a complex minus-sum game created to separate you from your $. You are, in fact, gambling with your retirement, pensions and 401k, just as if you were at the slot machines at Las Vegas.

You can only win if you figure out a way to beat the system.

But let me repeat this: You can't beat the system. There is no mathematical or scientific formula that exists that will make $ for *players* as a whole over time. It's impossible. The markets promote the winners but need the losers' $ to survive. It's a mathematical fact that *players* wind up with less $ at the end of every day than they started with. *Players* are the only ones taking $ out of their pockets and purchasing shares and contracts as part of the system. Brokers and exchanges are taking $ out of the system and putting it in their pockets.

It gets increasingly worse when you factor in the advantages that the *player* doesn't have. These include insider trading and information, CEO stock options, seats on the exchange, broker manipulation of stock prices, naked short-selling, and other factors.

Why "Crazyman's Economics" isn't promoting any way to "beat the system"
Simple: there isn't one. You think there are, and people write and refer to books on how they and others have succeeded in the markets. But it's a lie. They're

famous for using the Eagle's Eye view to show a few examples where their system made people $. However, here's the key: they don't show you complete statistics and don't provide a full accounting of *players*' $ because they don't have to. They never show what would have happened if you had applied the system consistently. If you were to test these methods, you'll find that in the long run, none of them work over time. Why? It's a minus-sum game. The idea that any book, program, seminar, or broker can promote a winning system without providing illegal inside information is a waste of your $ and energy. The few who make $ are no more significant to you as a *player* than your neighbor winning the lottery.

The Eagle's Eye view
I use the eagle as an example because, when an eagle is soaring above the ground, it can see everything before it. However, when they see their food, they focus intently on only that, ignoring everything else around. This single-minded focus is a strength for the eagle hunting for a meal but a weakness for *players* being deceived by brokers. By focusing on the Eagle's Eye view, brokers can draw on antidotal evidence show you individual cases to manipulate you to believe whatever it is they want to sell you. They won't tell you that the masses lose $. They won't produce a record of *players*' $ or where the $ goes.

The MASTERS do a brilliant job in promoting the Eagle's Eye view in discussing the advantages of the markets. They will encourage the

Fat Cats – The parasites which survive benefit and thrive off of the system the MASTERS set up. They can be in the financial services industry, government, academia, the media, as well as the corporate world.

ongoing success of certain funds, or prop up the success of certain analysts, or create a reporting system that reflects only the performance of a select few stocks, which are constantly changing to reflect the best stocks. They also utilize incomplete information and manipulate statistics, which they can use to show great wealth and success to the select few that follow their complex system. But at the end of the day, you can't beat the system because it's a minus-sum

Let's look at the charts below. All four are simple examples of what would happen if you purchased stock in a publicly traded company.

Example 1
Player A purchased a share of stock from a company for $100

	(out of pocket $)		(in pocket $)
Player A	$ 100	sells to Player B for	$ 110
Player B	$ 110	sells to Player C for	$ 120
Player C	$ 120	sells to Player D for	$ 130
Player D	$ 130		
Total out of pocket			$ 460
Total in-pocket			$ 360
Total out of pocket			**-$ 100**

In this example, Player A, B and C all made $ (after fees and commissions), and Player D is -$130. *Players* as a whole are -$100 + expenses.

Example 2
Player A purchased a share of stock from a company for $100

	(out of pocket $)		(in pocket $)
Player A	$ 100	sells to Player B for	$ 90
Player B	$ 90	sells to Player C for	$ 80
Player C	$ 80	sells to Player D for	$ 70
Player D	$ 70		
Total out of pocket			$ 340
Total in-pocket			$ 240
Total out of pocket			**-$ 100**

In this example, all *players* have lost $. Player D is -$70. *Players* as a whole are -$100 + expenses.

Example 3
Player A purchased a share of stock from a company for $100

	(out of pocket $)		(in pocket $)
Player A	$100	sells to Player B for	$100
Player B	$100	sells to Player C for	$100
Player C	$100	sells to Player D for	$100
Player D	$100		
Total out of pocket			$400
Total in-pocket			$300
Total out of pocket			**-$100**

In this example, all four *players* lost $ once you take out fees and commissions. The broker would avoid showing you this, but if he did, he would claim this is a zero-sum gain, but in fact, it is a minus-sum game. And the company got the $, and Player D is -$100. *Players* as a whole are -$100 + expenses.

Example 4
Player A purchased a share of stock from a company for $100

	(out of pocket $)		(in pocket $)
Player A	$100	sells to Player B for	$ 90
Player B	$ 90	sells to Player C for	$100
Player C	$100	sells to Player D for	$ 90
Player D	$ 90		
Total out of pocket			$380
Total in-pocket			$280
Total out of pocket			**-$100**

In this example, Player B makes $10, but Player A, C and D are minus $110 (plus added fees and commissions). When the broker explains this, he would show that Player B made $10, and Player D has a $90 value. *Players* as a whole are -$100 + expenses.

game, and *players* as a whole will lose $. Now, as you can see, brokers can use the Eagle's Eye view to highlight the message they want to use to keep *players* involved, although the bottom line is that *players* as a whole are losing $

Remember, if one *player* is making $, it's at the expense of one or more *players* losing money. And, as I discussed, when

(-$) – Every time you see this term, this means that $ is leaving your pockets and going into the pockets of the Fat Cats.

Crazyman $ays:
"The Fat Cats believe if it's legal then it's ethical."

you factor in fees, commissions, and taxes, it becomes a minus-sum game for *players.* The more you play, the worse it gets.

You can't beat the system because the system itself is designed against you. And yes, five percent will make $, and some will even make a lot of $. But the winners who make the five percent are paid for by the other 95 percent of *players.* Ask yourself who those people are that are losing $ so that the *player* makes $. Is it a rich guy in a mansion who doesn't care if he's losing $? No, in this day and age, it's likely your 401 (k) or pension plan that is losing $. The only sure thing about trying different ways to beat the system is the motion takes $ out of the pockets of *players* (-$) and puts it into the pockets of Fat Cats.

You have been taught to believe that with a book, newsletter, seminar, or financial advisor, you can beat the system and be a financial winner. The thing you need to recognize about these sales pitches is that they are constructed in a rhythmic pattern. They lead you through an explanation of the markets, and then sell you on why their specific system is the best one to win $. They show you examples of people who have successfully used the system, charts that highlight how the system works, and a plea that you act now to avoid being left out of this "sure thing." What they leave out is complete statistics, the stories of those who lost $, and any true statements that they have no more knowledge of the markets than anyone else.

The people who produce and promote these programs have, in essence, figured

out the only way to beat the system:
They get you to buy them and create a
consistent flow of $ into their pockets
that the markets cannot provide. In
return, these programs advance the
perception that the system can be beaten
and that they are designed in the best
interest of the *players*. As long as
everyone is playing by the rules, they
don't feel like to unethical it's take
advantage of the con to put your $ in
their pockets. But they know you can't
beat the system.

**Why good information told to too many
people becomes bad information**
Let's say you went to a poker game
knowing that the cards were marked. What
do you do? Well, you could use that
information to your advantage, and as
long as you didn't tell anyone, that is good
information. It's not ethical and I don't
recommend it, but it's part of my overall
point. Now, if you told everyone that the
cards were marked, then it goes back to an
equal playing ground, and it's no longer
good information. It's the same way with
the markets, it's possible one guy could
beat the system for a while, but as soon as
other *players* find out, it loses its value.
Think of that the next time you see a book
on how to beat the markets

As the old saying goes, "If three people
can keep a secret, it's because two of
them are dead." Consequently, if there
were some magic formula to beat the
markets, a few people could only benefit
from it for a short period of time. No
matter how good it is, when the masses
find out about it, it's back to an equal
playing field, and a minus-sum game.
You can never produce more winners

than losers, it's impossible.

You can't beat the system. A few do, but it helps to have inside information, participate in some type of illegal (or ethically-questionable) market manipulation, or have special advantages such as having a seat on the exchange. The only sure winners are the brokers and exchanges who generate fees and commissions. So the MASTERS keep a relentless focus on the Eagle's Eye view to keep *players* rooted in the game.

If you think that you can beat the system because you believe the markets are regulated and overseen by commissions that ensure fair play, consider this: the markets are all self-regulated. That means that the fox has been put in charge of the hen house. These regulatory agencies exist to establish and enforce rules merely to ensure fair play. They are not concerned with protecting the *players* from the organizations, but to protect organizations from the *players*.

The true role of regulatory commissions for the stock market and commodity markets are to:
▶ ensure the exchanges are successful;
▶ ensure the winners get their $;
▶ ensure the losers can't hold the brokers or exchanges liable;
▶ ensure the brokers and exchanges are not required to keep any records negative to their success.

It's up to the regulatory commissions to keep the markets functioning, because they don't survive because *players* are making $. They survive because *players* are losing $. Winners in the markets attract losers, and the markets survive on the losers. But the markets don't want to promote the fact that they need losers to survive. Without new *players*, the lights would go out. And without new blood, the system would collapse.

This is the reason the exchanges and brokerage firms do not keep or release any meaningful statistics that track *players* $. If the public had access to this information, they would see that it is impossible to beat the system, and they would see the vast amounts of $ that is funneled every day from the pockets of *players* (-$) into the pockets of the Fat Cats.

Bottom line: You can't beat the system.
(Got it?)

Chapter Two:
— Wall Street, the exchanges and casinos are all gambling facilities —

Folks, the stock market and commodity markets are gambling facilities, nothing more and nothing less. It's difficult to wrap our minds around the fact that the markets are something other than straight gambling. The truth is that Wall Street, the mercantile exchanges, and others are all gambling facilities as much as any casino in Las Vegas. They all operate under self-regulated rules, but the difference is that exchanges have to market themselves to the public as something they are not in order to draw new *players*.

Why do you gamble?
▶ You like predicting a non-predictable.
▶ You like to make a lot of $ with a little $ with no effort.
▶ You like to win.
▶ You think it's your only hope to ever accumulate financial security.
▶ It proves to others that you are willing to take a risk.
▶ It proves you are right, know what you are talking about, and are willing to put something of value at risk to prove it.
▶ You like to beat the odds.
▶ You like bragging rights/superiority/ self-esteem.
▶ You gamble to lose to increase the euphoria of winning.

Crazyman $ays:
"Losing is the foreplay
of winning."

▶ You, unfortunately, need to feed an addiction.

▶ The psychology makes it harder to walk away.

Casinos are promoted as pure entertainment, with no reason to promote themselves as something other than what they are. The markets, however, are promoted as performing an important business function with a vital economic value. In a casino, you are playing games that are marketed as a fun activity. There is no value attached to the games themselves. You know that you are gambling, and the name of the game is insignificant. A poker game is a poker game. Roulette, craps, blackjack...they're just games (they have no economic value to society).

Las Vegas never denies that the casinos are primarily gambling facilities. Even with the best restaurants, star-studded shows, and luxurious amenities, you know up front these are available to enhance the gambling environment to bring your $ into the specific casino. You may enjoy these activities, but try as you might, you are not going to hide the fact that you are at a casino to gamble.

Crazyman $ays:
"Gambling involves risking
something of value in
hopes of gaining something
of more value on a non-
predictable outcome,
with the odds favoring
the house and/or
your opponent."

To camouflage the market's reality of gambling, the MASTERS needed to convince the public that they were actually investing to enhance their savings and promote the economy of the United States. This is a formidable task. The MASTERS had to circumvent all of the entertainment and amenities that casinos offer and change your mindset to get you to believe that the stock market and commodity markets are a business function vital to everyone's well-being. You trust that you're investing because you've been convinced the games are a legitimate financial venture.

To get you to believe you're investing, the exchanges had to attach something of value to the names of the games. They took symbols that we believed were vital to our economy and used them as titles on their games (stock names, commodities, etc.). This allowed them to seduce the public into thinking they were investing in something of substance. In reality, they'd merely changed the title of the games, and it's still the same gambling games as Las Vegas. Either way, the key thing to remember is that the main element of all the games is that *players* are trying to predict an unpredictable. And the odds are stacked in favor of the house.

A major difference between gambling at a casino and gambling in the markets is that the markets present advantages to an elite few that the average *player* doesn't have. An elite few have access to inside information, a seat on the exchange, the ability to act on information instantly as opposed to when it hits the public, and access to information that the public doesn't receive. Some of this is legal, some not. All of these advantages results in an increase in the odds in favor of the Fat Cats.

There is a strong natural tendency for you as a *player* to ignore your losses and focus on your winnings. Casinos encourage this tendency by making sure

Crazyman $ays:
"Players dismiss their
losses and brag about
their winnings."

Crazyman $ays:
"Thinking about winning
is how we get trapped
into losing."

that every quarter that's won in a slot machine causes lights to blink and makes its own little jingle in the metal tray. Seeing all the lights and hearing all the clinking, it's not hard to get the impression that everyone's winning. If you watch the floor of the New York Stock Exchanges, with all of the yelling and running around and the flashing lights and the stock ticker, one cannot help but be caught up in the excitement thinking that fortunes are being made on the floor.

But losses are mostly silent.

So, while casinos are up front on the fact that they are gambling facilities, the MASTERS camouflage their motives through manipulation and conditioning in order to convince you that you are investing, trading, hedging, or speculating...anything else but gambling. They take advantage of the fact that you are searching for security to build a solid financial future for your family and your country.

In Las Vegas, *players* are told the odds in advance and even the most novice *player* understands that if you gamble long enough, the house will win. In the markets, you are not told the odds, only that there is risk involved. This risk is sugar-coated by the allure of winning by following the newest system.

The stock market convinces you that investing in companies is a manageable risk when you are actually gambling against other *players* in order to get your $ back. In the commodities market, you are told you are participating in a program that helps determine market prices, when in fact, you are gambling, trying to outguess other *players*. The key factor they all have in common is that they serve the primary goal of the MASTERS to keep your $ in motion while creating no products or services in return.

Let me ask you a question, why do Las Vegas bookmakers create the betting lines for a football game? It's not to predict an accurate outcome for the selected game (or there wouldn't be the 1/2 in the lines), but simply to get *players* to bet equally on both teams. This is also why betting lines are adjusted from the point the betting line is established to right before the game starts. Bookmakers will adjust the line to increase the bets on one side or the other to balance them out. This ensures that despite the payout, Vegas wins almost every time.

As a comparison, the betting lines, stock market, and commodity market prices are all affected by outside and unpredictable forces, whether it is the earnings report for a company, the weather forecast for a commodity, or an injury report for a football game.

In fact, if you line up Wall Street, the commodity markets, and casinos side-by-side for comparison, you'll see that they have nine things in common.

The MASTERS have learned that your search for security is your greatest weakness. As a society, people are willing to ignore logic and facts for a chance to gain financial security. That is the whole motivation around the lottery.

The elements that casinos, Wall Street and the commodities market have in common:

Element	Casinos	Stock Market	Commodity Markets
From simple to complex games	Slot machines to baccarat and horse racing, spending hours studying trends and charts	Simple stock purchase to those who spend hours/day studying the myriad of information/charts/graphs in order to make an educated guess	Simple contracts to studying complex formulas affecting the circumstances of the contract
How they separate *players* from their $	Players trade their $ for chips	Players trade their $ for shares	Players trade their $ for contracts
You have to guarantee *players* get their $	Casinos guarantee they will buy players chips back for the agreed value of the chips	If *players* sell their shares, the Exchange will make sure they get their $	Exchanges collect the $ up front in the form of 'margin $' and pays the winners from this fund.
Losing is the foreplay of winning	Players play games, losing more than they win, but hoping to win big. Players have to lose in order to get the thrill out of winning.	Players buy and sell stocks, losing more than they win, but hoping to win big. Players have to lose in order to get the thrill out of winning.	Players buy and sell contracts, losing more than they win, but hoping to win big. Players have to lose in order to get the thrill out of winning.
Players do not like to place their $ down once and walk away	Players like to stay in the game. The games are all designed to play over and over again. The system is set up to buy and sell by the second	Players like to stay in the game. The games are all designed to play over and over again. The system is set up to buy and sell by the second	Players like to stay in the game. The games are all designed to play over and over again. The system is set up to buy and sell by the second
Players risk something of value in a game	Players trade $ for chips	Players trade $ for shares	Players trade $ for a commodities contract
A self-regulatory system in place	Gambling Commissions for each state that allows legalized gambling. (example: Nevada Gaming Commission, NGC)	Security and Exchange Commission (SEC)	National Futures Association (NFA), The Commodity Futures Trading Commission (CFTA) & others
Have no legal recourse if *players* lose their $	All encouragement to participate in their games is followed by disclaimers that say that *players* are responsible for their losses, based on rules written by the regulatory commissions	All encouragement to participate in their games is followed by disclaimers that say that *players* are responsible for their losses, based on rules written by the regulatory commissions	All encouragement to participate in their games is followed by disclaimers that say that *players* are responsible for their losses, based on rules written by the regulatory commissions
Not required to keep records that will be a negative to the organizations	Casinos are not required to keep records that state how many *players* lost $ or how much	Exchanges are not required to keep records on how the *players*' $ is divided. The brokers are not required to keep performance records	Exchanges are not required to keep records on how the *players*' $ is divided. The brokers are not required to keep performance records

I've personally never seen a doctor scratching off a lottery ticket, but I've seen plenty of poor folks struggling to make ends meet pay $ for a one-in-millions chance at financial security.

The MASTERS know that when you are considering participating in a 401k or pension plan, you are seeking a way to ensure financial security for you and your family. It's easy for brokers to pull you into the web when you want to believe what they have to sell. You don't want to believe you're gambling. You want to believe in sure things. So you give over your $ hoping the broker, promises of a "sure thing" will turn out to be a certainty. But you're involved in predicting an unpredictable, so there is no "sure thing."

Brokers are trained to sell you stocks, bonds, commodities, whatever gambling game you want to play to get your $ in motion. They're taught to convince you to downplay the risk and follow their advice to win $ in the markets. Of course it's a gamble, they'll say, but by (fill in the blank), you will make $. Of course they talk about the risks, but only as an example of *players* who listened to bad advice (or even worse) tried to play the markets on their own.

That Vegas and the markets constantly need to attract new *players* is the key. All three produce 95 percent losers to winners, and losers are what fuel the system. In trying to outsmart the system, we are drawn into the system, and the system itself is designed to create losers to survive.

Crazyman $ays:
"Our search for security is the greatest threat to our freedoms."

The difference is that Las Vegas at least tells *players* the odds up front, and brings *players* back for the entertainment (and addiction) aspects. Both the stock market and commodities market avoid the negative comparisons to gambling by promoting it as investing. *Players* are rarely aware of the odds of winning or losing, only that there is some risk involved.

Either way, the fact is that *players* are gambling in a minus-sum game against fellow *players* by trying to predict an unpredictable for financial gain. It's OK to gamble as long as you know the odds and risks going in. The fact that the stock market and the commodity markets don't tell you the odds makes it easy to conclude that casinos are the most legitimate of the three.

Chapter Three:
— Motion (the MASTERS' greatest asset and the players' greatest enemy) —

What is motion in relation to the markets, and why is it important? Every time you as a *player* purchase a share of stock, make changes in a mutual fund, or buy and sell commodity contracts, motion is created. Each time motion occurs, brokers and exchanges collect a cut. If a broker wants to make a large commission, he needs to generate as much motion as possible. The more motion that is created, the more successful the exchanges are. You'll notice that there is no mention of your success with your investments playing into this equation. Brokers and exchanges do not care if your investments are successful or not, only that you keep investing.

It's motion that takes investing from a zero-sum gain to a minus-sum game. Brokers' and exchanges' main goal is to get your $ as a *player* into motion and keep it in motion. It's important that you remember this. Each time you initiate activity in the markets, motion is created, and fees and commissions are produced. And this motion takes $ from the pockets of *players* (-$) and puts $ in the pockets of Fat Cats. Once you enter the game, every time you buy and sell stocks or commodities, you are

Crazyman $ays:
"Motion takes $ out of the pockets of players and puts it in the pockets of the Fat Cats."

Warren Buffett $ays: "For investors as a whole, returns decrease as motion increases."

just shuffling $ among *players*. Each transaction costs you real $ in fees and commissions to brokers and exchanges. That produces a negative cash flow (-$). In return, you get a piece of paper with published value. This provides a false sense of security since published value is the greatest illusion of actual wealth. What you are actually doing is transferring real cash in exchange for pretend $.

Now you may believe that fees and commissions are the price of doing business and should not counted in whether you make $ or lose $, but look at this as a large spinning wheel. Every time the wheel turns, a penny falls off. The more turns, the more pennies fall off into the Fat Cats' pockets. Doesn't sound like much until you realize the wheel turns millions of times every day the markets are open.

Therefore, the markets need that wheel spinning constantly to stay in business.

What keeps the wheel spinning (motion) for the Fat Cats?
1. Constantly changing prices without using a solid mathematical or scientific formula,
2. The ability to buy and sell by the second which creates volatility in the markets,
3. The volatility creates insecurity, which draws you back into the system by enticing *players* to act,
4. This action accelerates motion,
5. The need to constantly find new *players* or new blood.

The MASTERS recognize our need for security and design their entire promotional campaign around providing a stable financial future that is almost cruel in its deception. They created a process which takes advantage of *players'* insecurity by creating volatility, which accelerates motion, which encourages *players* to buy and sell to prevent being caught in a losing position. Fighting to gain or regain financial security, it puts *players* farther in debt. This plays right into their hands.

We know the MASTERS have designed and developed this system, and they need the brokers to find new *players* and keep the losers from leaving the market. You are their target, and they have to convince you that they are working on your behalf. They need to create a unique level of trust that permits you to hand over your $ to them without question.

Without *players* creating the motion, the markets would fail. The brokers and exchanges would go out of business. What a process! The MASTERS have created a whirlwind of confusion and motion to separate their clients from trillions of $ of cash over the years and into their own pockets. All this in return for issuing pieces of paper with no actual value, and yet the public believes they're rich.

What draws players to the game of the markets?
Players are pulled into the game by the opportunity of taking a little $ and turning it into a lot of $ quickly without

effort. This is done by constantly changing prices and buying and selling by the second, which are the main components of the stock market and commodities market.

There are those who buy into the dream that they can manipulate the markets to win big. For example: This is a simple formula of how a *player* can use the pyramid of wealth formula to quickly turn their $ once they invest in the market:

The significance of the formula is that on a Certificate of Deposit, or bonds you would purchase at a bank, the rate of return is five percent for the year. In the markets, *players* have the possibility of making a ten percent return in a day, multiplied by 365 days. The returns could be monumental if everything worked in favor of the *player*.

Plug even the smallest number and do the math, and you can see how a *player* can turn a little $ into a lot of $ quickly.

Pyramid
of
wealth formula

The percentage of
$ gained times (x)
the number of trades per day
times (x) 365 days

If you have 1% gain x
10 trades per day=10% return
per day x 365 days
= 3,650% return on investment.

Margins in the commodity markets

In the commodity markets, margin $ are used as an added incentive *players* have to take a risk. A margin is like a down payment, by only putting down a portion of the true value of the contract as risk, which averages out to approximately 1/20th.

Putting up 1/20th of the value of a commodity allows *players* the possibility to make 20 times return of its true value. This incentive allows *players* to believe they can turn a little $ into a lot of $ quickly without effort.

Now, I'll show you the same pyramid of wealth formula using margin $:

Margin call – When the margin posted in the margin account is below the minimum margin requirement, the broker or exchange issues a call for more $ to be put into the account. The *player* now either has to increase the margin $ that he has deposited, or he can settle his contract.

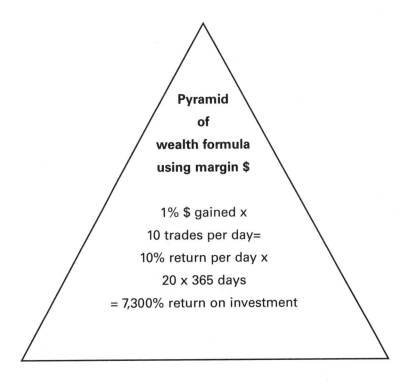

Pyramid
of
wealth formula
using margin $

1% $ gained x
10 trades per day=
10% return per day x
20 x 365 days
= 7,300% return on investment

Crazyman $ays:
"With all things being
equal, all players will lose
$ in time."

With margins, *players* are in the position of risking only 1/20th of the amount to make a possible 7,300% return-on-investment, if they are making a ten percent return in a day, multiplied by 365 days. The returns could be monumental, if everything worked in favor of the *player*.

Margins also make it possible to sell a commodities contract you purchased and buy back more than you sold with the same $. For example, if a corn contract is $2.00, and margins required are 1/20th, you pay 10 cents in margin $ to buy a bushel of corn ($2.00 divided by 20 = 10 cents). If corn goes up 10 cents, you can sell it for 20 cents, and take the 20 cents and buy two bushels of corn for the initial investment of 10 cents.

The obvious downfall is that you could make an incorrect prediction, or the exchange could ask you to contribute more $ (known as a "margin call") and you could be in serious financial difficulty. Margins should be eliminated in the commodity markets, period. If a *player* wants to take a risk on a contract, they should be required to put up all of the risk.

The power of "doubling up"
Despite the obvious risks, it's this mental process of doubling up on winnings which brings *players* into the game. To show you the power of doubling up, let's use the "child's birthday" scenario. Let's say you put $1 into your child's savings account on their 1st birthday, and you doubled it to $2 on their 2nd birthday and $4 on their 3rd, birthday, and so on,

this is what would happen by the time your child was 21 years old:

Contribute $1 at age 1	
Age 2 $2	Age 3 $4
Age 4 $8	Age 5 $16
Age 6 $32	Age 7 $64
Age 8 $128	Age 9 $256
Age 10 $512	Age 11 $1024
Age 12 $2048	Age 13 $4096
Age 14 $8192	Age 15 $16,384
Age 16 $32,768	Age 17 $65,536
Age 18 $131,072	Age 19 $262,144
Age 20 $524,288	Age 21 $1,048,576

Now, imagine if you can use margin $ to do this over the course of several hours, days or weeks, instead of years? This is a great deal as long as prices work in your favor. But there are no guarantees or formulas either way. It's this appeal of almost instant wealth that draws *players* into the game and creates the motion. And this motion takes $ out of the pockets of *players* (-$) and puts $ into the pockets of Fat Cats and ultimately is the downfall of the *players*. The wins can be substantial, the losses devastating.

The only constant in keeping *players'* $ in motion is that the prices continually change, brokers collect their commissions, exchanges collect their fees, and the government collects taxes on any gains. Remember that the sole purpose of the MASTERS is to keep your $ in constant motion, and by keeping it in motion, this will result in a minus-sum game for *players* as a whole.

Now, this is a brilliant strategy of the MASTERS. Due to the fees and commissions produced with each motion generated. If you play long enough, the Fat Cats will wind up with all *players'* $ in time.

Chapter Four:
— Published value, perceived value and outperformed —

If you have share of stock with published value, you have no $, with no promise of real $ to back it up. We're living in a world where we are relying on an increasing level on published value with no promise to pay with no $ to back it up! Millions of times a day, *players* in the markets trade real $ in return for a piece of paper to use to gamble with other *players*. All you've done is pay a cover charge to play the MASTERS game. The person holding the paper has no real $ until someone decides to buy your paper. More importantly, the paper has no real value outside of the markets.

Crazyman $ays:
"Published value and perceived value are the greatest illusions of actual wealth."

Here's what you need to know about published value:
▶ Shares of stock are as valuable as a piece of paper;
▶ The guy holding the paper has no $ and never will as long as he's holding the paper;
▶ The actual value of the share is ZERO;
▶ There is no $ to back up the shares and no guarantee that you will find a buyer;
▶ Unlike casino chips, there's no place to turn a share back in for $;

▶ Until the share is removed from,
there will always be someone
holding the bag;
▶ Ninety-nine percent of all listed
shares will eventually wind up in the
dumpster;
▶ The average life of a publicly traded
company is eight years.

The price listed for the individual share is
what is called "published value." When
the share is issued from the company,
the company keeps the $ and gives you a
piece of paper. The piece of paper is only
good to trade among *players* and
generate $ for the Fat Cats until it is
removed from trading. It has no real
value; it's only based on the perception
of the buyers and sellers. Until you sell
your shares, you have nothing of value.
It's like holding chips in Vegas and the
casino won't buy them back. Casino
chips have value and shares do not.
Ninety-nine percent of the paper you
hold will wind up in the dumpster. It's up
to you whether you are the one throwing
it away.

You saw a small sample of this during
the dot-com crash earlier this decade
which saw scores of people who were
millionaires on paper one day broke or
millions of dollars in debt the next when
the published value of their stock went in
the toilet. The truth is they were broke on
both days; it was only their published
value which changed.

Let's revisit the example again of how the
MASTERS use published value and
perceived value in the stock market:

Example 1
Player A purchased a share of stock from a company for $100

	(out of pocket $)		(in pocket $)
Player A	$100	sells to Player B for	$110
Player B	$110	sells to Player C for	$120
Player C	$120	sells to Player D for	$130
Player D	$130		
Total out of pocket	$460		
Total in-pocket			$360
Total out of pocket		**-$**	**100**

In this example, Player A, B and C all made $ (after fees and commissions), and Player D is -$130. *Players* as a whole are -$100 + expenses.

Example 2
Player A purchased a share of stock from a company for $100

	(out of pocket $)		(in pocket $)
Player A	$100	sells to Player B for	$90
Player B	$90	sells to Player C for	$80
Player C	$80	sells to Player D for	$70
Player D	$70		
Total out of pocket	$340		
Total in-pocket			$240
Total out of pocket			**-$100**

In this example, all *players* have lost $. Player D is -$70. *Players* as a whole are -$100 + expenses.

Example 3
Player A purchased a share of stock from a company for $100

	(out of pocket $)		(in pocket $)
Player A	$100	sells to Player B for	$100
Player B	$100	sells to Player C for	$100
Player C	$100	sells to Player D for	$100
Player D	$100		
Total out of pocket	$400		
Total in-pocket			$300
Total out of pocket			**-$100**

In this example, all four *players* lost $ once you take out fees and commissions. The broker would avoid showing you this, but if he did, he would claim this is a zero-sum gain, but in fact, it is a minus-sum game. And the company got the $, and Player D is -$100. *Players* as a whole are -$100 + expenses.

Example 4

Player A purchased a share of stock from a company for $100

	(out of pocket $)		(in pocket $)
Player A	$100	sells to Player B for	$ 90
Player B	$ 90	sells to Player C for	$100
Player C	$100	sells to Player D for	$ 90
Player D	$ 90		
Total out of pocket	$380		
Total in-pocket			$280
Total out of pocket			**-$100**

In this example, Player B makes $10, but Player A, C and D are minus $110 (plus added fees and commissions). When the broker explains this, he would show that Player B made $10, and Player D has a $90 value. *Players* as a whole are -$100 + expenses.

Player D represents the millions of *players* in this country that hold approximately $15 Trillion of published value stocks today. They have paper worth, but no cash $ in pocket. And what will happen to all of the Player D's of the world? They will be replaced with Player E, and so on. And that process continues to create motion. And eventually, the share will float among *players* until it is removed from trading. When that happens, the last player (D, E or whoever) will be holding an empty bag.

The danger we're facing now is that millions of everyday Americans with retirement plans and pensions are in the same boat. One day their published and perceived value will be exposed as being worthless pieces of paper, and I would like to prevent this from happening to you as it happened to me at Eastern Airlines.

If you learn nothing else from this book, I would like you to take out of "Crazyman's Economics" the understanding that the terms "published value," "perceived value" and "outperformed" are words of illusion with no real value. They give you a positive outlook on a negative situation, but nothing to sink your teeth into.

You see, unless you have actual cash in your pocket, what you have listed on a piece of paper is just that—a piece of paper. Published value is just an assigned value, and it has no real value until you find someone to give you $ in return for the paper. Perceived value is just how valuable you think you are.

If you look at these three terms:
▶ They do not represent true value;
▶ Brokers use these terms to deceive *players* and avoid accountability;
▶ Hearing them can give *players* a positive outlook on a negative situation.

Real value vs. published value/perceived value

If your broker told you that your portfolio had a published value of a million dollars and had outperformed the S&P 500®, you would think you were a millionaire. Except the paper you hold cannot be turned into real $. All you can do is move it from one *player* to another. The paper you hold has an unpredictable selling price. Until you find a buyer, your pockets are as empty as they were that morning. Now, go to the grocery store and buy bread and milk with your published value.

You have perceived value that you are a millionaire, but take some shares of stock to go to a fast food restaurant and try to

Published value – The greatest illusion of actual wealth. It only has value if you can find a buyer.

Perceived value – Accepting and acting on your belief that your published value is legitimate.

Outperformed – A random determination of performance, with no true point of reference.

Consider this:

If you spent a million dollars a day, you would be well over **3,000 years old** before you spent a trillion dollars.

buy lunch. Or take a commodities contract to the bank and see if they'll give you a loan. What you hold in your hand is perceived value. You perceive you have $ from the published value of the paper, but you can't trade that paper for anything of value.

The illusion the MASTERS created is perceived value which is the $ you imagine you can redeem for something, but does not exist. The deception is published value which is the value assigned by society. Both are illusions of actual wealth. You cannot go to the grocery store and buy food with your perceived or published value. The only way you as a *player* can know your true wealth at the end of the day is the actual $ you have in your pocket.

The impact of how perceived value and published value is a ticking time-bomb cannot be overstated. As of this writing, there is approximately $300 trillion of outstanding derivative contracts, as well as approximately $16 trillion in published value of outstanding stock. This is an astonishing concept, because it's well beyond the amount of $ that can be printed, spent or kept. The fact is that the $ doesn't exist. It can't exist and won't ever exist in the future. It's a numbers game and paper shuffle among *players*. The simple fact is that the MASTERS have convinced you that having published value means real $ is involved. But it's a lie. The $ isn't there. The only $ generated goes from your pocket (-$) to the pockets of the Fat Cats. They now have real $, and you have a piece of paper. Do you still think brokers are working in your best interests?

As we're learning, *players* are being conned into participating in a minus-sum game played with paper circulating among *players* until the paper finally goes out of circulation. Eventually the motion will eat it up, or the paper will lose its value. And the hundreds of trillions of dollars in outstanding stock and commodities contracts create a vast wasteland of perceived value with no cash to back it up.

When a stock is issued, it is assigned in a computer system with the name of the shareholder attached to it.

The only two ways you can remove an issued stock share:
1. The company buys it back (only happens approximately one percent of the time);
2. The company/share is removed from trading.

The only $ generated to *players* is when the company buys back its shares, which only happens approximately one percent of the time. It's not like taking your T-bill or Certificate of Deposit to the bank and the bank paying you the value of the paper. In that case, you've retired the paper. Now, the difference is that companies retiring a share only happens about one percent of the time. The other 99 percent remains out there, shuffling between *players*. Once again, there is no $ there. It is a perceived value.

So, real $ is separated from *players*, without creating a product or service and transferred to a few parasitic Fat Cats. This process increases the standard of living for these parasites by having actual $, and decreases the standard of living for the *players*, by transferring real wealth for published wealth. This process results in a negative pull on the economy by taking disposable income from the public and funneling it to the Fat Cats. But, you have satisfied the goal of the MASTERS by placing your $ in motion. And by keeping that $ in motion the MASTERS continue to skim your $ off the top and create NOTHING in return.

Outperformed what (or who)?
Outperformed is simple in its deception. You can have two losers, and one outperformed the other. You can have two winners, and one outperformed the other. If you didn't know what you were performing against, and you didn't include all of the statistics, the word has absolutely no value.

Here are a few examples: Your broker is pushing you to buy shares in Company A because it outperformed market expectations for the last quarter. Now, Company A was expected to lose $50 million and it only lost $45 million so it outperformed expectations, even though they lost $45 million.

Example two: Company B claims it outperformed Company A, and Company B loses $40 million. Company B outperformed Company A by 20%, yet they both lost $.

A makes $1,000 and B makes $1,001. B outperformed A, but the gain is insignificant.

Outperformed can mean anything. Without full disclosure and

accountability, the broker is avoiding giving you honest statistics. They make it appear that outperformed is an improvement over a negative, or an improvement over a positive. It makes a poor or negative situation look like a positive.

The brilliance of all of these terms is that *players* are convinced to pay a "cover charge" of real $ in return for an issued piece of paper that allows you to play the MASTERS game of gambling. You are now among those who are out $15 trillion and the paper is shuffling between *players*. Look at the charts and see that there is no $ created in the motion, it just puts *players,* as a whole deeper in debt.

I asked my banker at the diner if I were to go to the bank in the investment department and have them draw me up an investment proposal. Now, if I were to take that proposal to the loan department and see if they'll give you a loan based on that investment proposal? He said they wouldn't give me a loan based on their recommendations.

When you review your financial reports, remember the terms "published value," "perceived value," and "outperformed," and see if they appear in your broker's vocabulary. If they do, you're in danger of being one of the ones who are left holding the bag when it's time to collect your retirement or pension.

Chapter Five:
— What you think the stock market is, and what it really is —

Here's a story that was told to me: Once upon a time in a village, a man appeared and announced to the villagers that he would buy monkeys for $10 each. The villagers, seeing that there were many monkeys around, went out to the forest and started catching them.

The man bought thousands of monkeys at $10, and as the supply started to diminish, the villagers stopped catching them. The man then announced that he would now buy monkeys for $20. This renewed the efforts of the villagers and they started catching monkeys again.

Soon, the supply diminished even further and people started going back to their farms. The offer increased to $25 for each monkey, but the supplies of monkeys were so scarce, that it was an effort to even see a monkey, let alone catch one.

The man then announced that he would buy monkeys for $50! However, since he had to return to the city on some business, his assistant would now buy on his behalf.

Crazyman $ays:
"Losing in the markets is like asking where all the 'white' went when the snow melted."

In the absence of the man, the assistant told the villagers, "Look at all of these monkeys in the big cage that the man has collected. I will sell them to you at $35 each, and when my boss returns from the city, you'll be able to sell them to him for $50 each."

The villagers rounded up all of their savings and bought all of the monkeys from the assistant.

They never saw the man or his assistant again, only monkeys everywhere they looked.

Now, you have a better understanding of how the stock market works.

I'm trying to get you to quit turning your $ over with blind confidence to a $ manager you believe has your best interest at heart. I feel I have to make you understand that what you've been trained to think the stock market is and what the reality is, are two separate things.

In my discussions with average people, this is what they think the stock market is:

▶ They think the stock market is a legitimate place to invest your $.
▶ They think all publicly traded companies make a profit.
▶ They think that, if they invest in those companies, they will share in their growth and profit.
▶ They think that the people who handle their $ are working in their best interests.

▶ They think they are securing their
  future through safe investing in a
  401k, pension, or retirement fund,
  with minimal risk.

▶ They think the price of shares are
  based on the financial report and
  performance of the company.

▶ They think that the system is so hard
  to understand, it's OK to hand over
  their $ in confidence to brokers or $
  managers.

▶ At that point, they walk away
  confidently thinking their retirement
  and investments are secure.

In fact, it's hard for most people to
believe the stock market is simply a
highly complex con game created,
developed and controlled by the
MASTERS. In order to keep it operating,
they need to make sure the company,
brokers, exchanges, and the government
gets their $. If you are making $ with
your 401k, retirement, or pension through
the stock market, that means that others
who may have the same retirement
plans are losing $. In a minus-sum
game, you must have more losers than
winners since it's the losers that support
the system.

As a *player*, your participation in the
markets consists of a piece of paper that
has published value. It is a contract
which protects the MASTERS from you
when you lose your $. It only guarantees
that everyone involved plays by the
rules. It holds no guarantees that you
can find a buyer, or that you will receive
cash $ in return for the buyer taking
possession of your paper.

In a majority of situations in which you purchase shares of stocks from a publicly traded company...

▶ the company receives free capital,
▶ the brokers and commissions make $ through commissions and fees,
▶ the IRS makes $ off of your winnings,
▶ all *players* as a whole lose $.

The system is set up by the MASTERS to benefit the Fat Cats at the expense of the *players*. Since I described a good deal as one in which all parties benefit, and *players* as a whole lose $, the market is not a good deal for all.

This has resulted in a process in which 95 percent of *players* lose $ with the only sure winners being the companies, brokers, and exchanges. If you don't believe me, show me the numbers that will disprove that claim. (I will save you some time, they don't exist.) And where does the $ come from if you make $? It comes from another *player*. We have been taught to ignore who these other *players* are. I've had people tell me when I ask them where their winnings come from in the market: "I don't care."

The fact is you should care, because the other *players* are your grandparents' savings, retirement funds, the pension of a widow, and *players* who trust the wrong people with their life savings. This is what they don't tell you, what they don't want you to know. Ask around. See who is losing $, and tell me if they live in a mansion or across the street from you.

The reality of the stock market is you're not investing

Consider my definition of investing as "a 100% possibility of everyone making $ based on the profit from the production of goods or services." The reality is that from the beginning, you are not investing. You are entering in a minus-sum game, in which at the end of each day, *players* as a whole have less $ in pocket than they started with. You are participating in a non-predictable, but the results are predictable...9 out of 10 *players* will lose $. You have satisfied the goal of the MASTERS by putting your $ in motion. The process of gambling has begun.

Let me walk you through this process: When a publicly traded company issues a share, the company receives your $ in return for the share and does not pay it back. Let's follow the progression and do the math. You pay a fee to a broker (- $), who then takes your $ and buys a share from a company (-$). The price you paid for paper and fees are non-refundable, and the company is no longer involved. The company's name provides a reference point for selling the shares at a later date, but there is no mathematical or scientific formula to determine the price of shares. What's important to know is that the price of the shares is not determined by any formula or company financial report but strictly by the mental state of the *players*. The buyer has to believe his $ is worth less than your share, and you have to think his $ is worth more than your paper. No matter how valuable you believe your share to be, unless you find someone to purchase it, the price is completely negotiable. The

The process
of buying stocks

Player A gives $ to a broker

▼

Broker charges fee and gets
commission for trade (-$)

▼

Broker gives $ to exchange

▼

Exchange gets a fee (-$)

▼

Exchange then issues a share

▼

The company gets the $, which
they don't pay back (-$)

▼

Exchange has your share with
your name on it

▼

There is no guarantee you can
sell your share, no guaranteed
price. The share has a non-
predictable selling price

▼

If Player A wants their $ back,
they have to pay a broker to sell
the share to Player B

▼

The broker collects fees and
commissions (-$). The price
Player B pays is based totally
on what the buyer is willing to
pay. There's no way to
rationalize the price, it's all
subjective

▼

Player B will sell to Player C,
Player C sells to Player D, and
so on...

▼

Each movement involves fees
and commissions paid to the
brokers and exchanges (-$). This
process will continue until the
shares are removed from the
exchange

▼

The last *player* is holding an
empty bag

▼

The last *player* has no
real $, and there is no $ to retire
the stock

moment the share is purchased, you have now bought something with a non-predictable selling price.

Back to the math: You have purchased the right to put your name on a piece of paper (share) which is turned over to the exchange for a fee (- $) to be put into motion. Every time that paper is in motion, this takes $ out of the pockets of *players* (-$) and puts $ in the pockets of Fat Cats. If you make $, that means one or more *players* has to lose $. It's impossible for 100% of *players* to make $. The chart to the left explains it the same way.

The last *player* is left holding the bag, and there's no $ to retire the stock. But he thinks he has real $. This is a good example of a *player* having published value which is the greatest illusion of actual wealth. There is approximately $15 trillion of outstanding stock and no $ in which to buy them back from *players*. *Players* think they are wealthy, but there's no $ there.

When a player thinks they're investing, they're actually:

▶ trying to turn a little $ into a lot of $ quickly without effort,

▶ trying to predict an unpredictable,

▶ giving the exchanges and brokers a cut every time the shares are in motion,

▶ buying and selling shares based on the mental process of the *players*, not on any mathematical or scientific formula,

▶ not performing a business function but trying to out-predict other *players*.

These are the classic definitions of gambling.

Make no mistake, the exchanges are gambling operations, and brokers are glorified bookies hustling *players* from all sides in order to keep your $ in motion so that they can get their fees and commissions. Consequently, they do not care if you win $ or lose $, only that your $ remains in motion.

You've been taught to believe that all large companies are $ making ventures. You believe that investing in something of value can result in sharing equally in its growth and profit. As a result, as a company sees an increase in profits, you should see an equal return in proportion. Dividends are supposed to be paid to the shareholders for the use of their $. This does not happen. The fact is the company keeps the $ up front when the stock is issued, and if one *player* makes $, it comes out of the pocket of another *player*. The company now has "free capital" to work with and is not obligated in any way to repay the *player*.

If a publicly traded company pays a dividend at all, it is usually after it decides to reinvest the profit back into the company (called "retained earnings"). This is at the discretion of the board of directors. If you factor in the $ that goes to the company, likely not to be returned, along with fees and commissions for each transaction, you are participating in a minus-sum game. Remember, the published value is determined by the perception of the buyer, not on any proven scientific or mathematical formula.

Reality: A company does not share its profits equally with *players*, and the average dividend they pay out is less than one percent.

Crazyman $ays:
"You don't have a place
to retire shares, only to
bury them."

If the company chooses not to pay dividends on the shares you have purchased, you have no chance of getting your original investment back from the company (only from selling the shares to another *player*). And even if you receive a two percent dividend return (the average is one-three percent), it would take 50 years to get your original investment back. Even the chances of this happening are very remote due to the fact that the average life span of a publicly traded company is only eight years.

The key is you are entering a negative cash flow. From the very beginning *players* pay their brokers a fee to give their $ to a company in exchange for issued shares of stocks. That is one negative cash flow (-$). The company doesn't pay back what the *player* put in. That's a negative cash flow (-$). The IRS taxes all *players'* winnings as capital gains. That's a negative cash flow (-$).

If one *player* makes $ off another *player*, the IRS taxes all your winnings, the exchanges collect their fees, and the brokers collect their commissions.

Reality: The stock market is not required to keep records tracking where *players* $ goes.

Here's an example:
A player buys shares of stock for $100,000 and
▼
sells them to another player for $200,000.
▼
He makes $100,000 profit, minus fees and commissions.
▼
Let's say for the sake of argument that he owes the
IRS a Capital Gains tax of 35 percent,
or $35,000, plus the exchange fees.
▼
He decides to purchase another $200,000 worth of stock,
▼
and the company goes broke,
▼
causing the player to lose all $200,000.
▼
He is only allowed to write off $3,000 that year against his losses.
▼
He lost all of his $ he had in the markets,
and still owes the government $32,000
in taxes for $ he no longer has.

Either way, this creates a positive cash flow to the government,
exchanges and brokers, and a minus-sum game to *players* as a
whole, no matter if you as a *player* win or lose.

However, if you lose $, the exchanges
still get their fees.

As a *player*, the only positive cash flow
you can have is through:
1. The company buying back the stock
   (which happens on average about
   one percent of the time)
2. The company pays a dividend (Some
   companies don't pay a dividend, and
   the ones that do pay an average of
   one-three percent.)

Remember: Once you give your $ to the
broker to give to that company, the $ is
gone. What you have in return is a piece
of paper with published value, the

greatest illusion of actual wealth. With
fees and commission paid to brokers and
exchanges, the only constant is that $
is transferred from your pocket (-$) to
the pockets of the Fat Cats. Each and
every time.

The feds have failed to hold the
exchanges accountable for investors' $
and let them regulate themselves. They
are supposed to be looking out for the
people, but they let the exchanges
regulate themselves. Name another
business that does not have a financial
accountability report.

There's no accountability to the system
without full disclosure tracking *players'*
$. This has allowed us to be drawn into
a minus-sum game in which we are
shuffling paper with no real value
among *players* while the Fat Cats get real
$ from the motion. And with the
propaganda that is bombarded on the
public daily, that's how *players* get
trapped into the system.

I have proven that you can't beat the
system, because the stock market is a
minus-sum game for the *players* from
the moment they hand over their $ to a
company. The best advice I can give is to
get the losers to quit losing. If they quit
losing, how can it be bad for the
economy? By taking your $ out of the
pockets of Fat Cats and investing it in
your community, it would be a positive
to all but a few bitter Fat Cats.

Chapter Six:
—What we think the commodities market is, and what it really is —

Many of the products you purchase on a daily basis have their prices determined by actions in the commodity markets. Commodity markets control prices of oil, corn, grain, soybeans, wheat, steel, and other basics listed. Even if you are not involved in the commodity markets as a *player*, you need to understand how they affect your everyday life and take $ out of the pockets of *players* (-$) and put $ in the pockets of Fat Cats.

The commodity markets are very complex in design. To describe the primary function of the commodity markets as they promote it in a few words is impossible. This is by design. Any businessman would not sign off on a program he doesn't understand. In your case, if you can't understand it, you can't criticize it or regulate it. They need to get rid of it.

Crazyman $ays:
"A commodity is a product (corn, oil, steel, etc.) which is part of our livelihood and has real value."

Here are the basics as they stand today: The exchanges tell you the commodity markets offer a vital economic function by providing an effective and efficient mechanism for the management of price risks. They also assert

that competitive price discovery has a main economic role and is a key economic benefit of futures trading. They have been popularized as a measure of supply and demand, as a vehicle for keeping prices low, always working in the consumers' best economic interests. It's not true.

If you don't understand that, that's fine, it's a deception anyway. Here's all you need to know: The commodity markets are pure gambling.

The goal of the *player* purchasing a contract is to sell it to make $. But from the beginning, he is entering a minus-sum game. Remember, a minus-sum game means that at the end of the day, all *players* have less $ than they started with. They are stuck with exchange fees (- $), broker commissions (- $) and taxes (-$).

Here's how it works: You pay a fee to a broker (- $), who then takes your margin $ and gives it to the exchange, and buys a contract (-$) with a specified delivery or settlement date (the end of the contract). The published price you paid for the contract was not determined by any mathematical or scientific formula. The process for establishing contract prices is based on the mental process of the *players* that involves an infinite number of factors. You've now purchased a contract with a non-predictable selling price. The process of gambling has begun.

In order to reconcile your contract, you have to pay a broker (- $) to sell or settle your contract on or before the settlement

Reality: You are entering into a game of chance called gambling.

Margin $ - Down payment the holder of a contract uses to cover the risk.

Process of buying commodity contracts

Player A gives margin $ to a broker to purchase a commodities contract.

Broker charges fee and gets commission for contract (-$).

Broker gives margin $ to exchange.

Exchange gets a fee (-$), and the margin $ is to cover losses if they occur (-$).

Exchange then issues a contract with a settlement date.

There is no guarantee you can sell your contact and no guaranteed price. The contract has a non-predictable selling price.

Player A is now in a high-risk situation, because from the moment he purchased the contract, the prices constantly change. If Player A wants to settle the contract, he has to pay a broker to sell or settle the contract on or before the settlement date.

The broker collects fees and commissions (-$) on the settlement. The price of settlement is based totally on what the buyer is willing to pay. There's no way to rationalize the price. It's all subjective. If the prices change enough opposite his position, Player A could lose his margin $, (-$) and if the prices keep changing, the exchange could call for more margin $ to cover losses.

date. Remember, the brokers and exchanges don't care if you as a *player* either made $ or lost $ on the contract, because they always make $ from the motion created by the contract. And it's this motion which takes $ out of the pockets of *players* (-$) and puts it in the pockets of Fat Cats.

When Player A settles the contract, if he made $, it came from the other *players'* margin $. If Player A lost $, it goes from his margin $ into the account of the other *player*, minus fees and commissions.

Let's review the process of purchasing commodities:

▶ *Players* are betting against each other trying to predict a non-predictable,

▶ The house (exchange) gets a cut on every transaction,

▶ The odds are stacked against the *players*,

▶ *Players* are participating in a minus-sum game,

▶ *Players* margin $ is held in escrow to guarante the winners get their $,

▶ *Players* as a whole can't beat the system.

Slot machines, roulette wheels, and craps are all games of chance risking something of value in an attempt to predict a non-predictable. By playing the commodities market, you are playing similar games except the names going around the wheel are corn and crude oil. Other games are named after absurd concepts like degree days. Titles of the games are insignificant as long as they draw *players* to the games. Buying and selling contracts in the commodity markets are no different than feeding coins into slot machines.

Each contract purchased is just another pull of the lever with the house always taking a cut. *Players* are not sharing wealth from the production of these commodities. They are simply participating in gambling games against other *players*.

This is gambling, no more or no less.

Here's how the MASTERS made it complex, and how the brokers market it to us:

▶ the use of weak and misleading words,

▶ the manipulation and lack of statistics,

▶ the changing of the label of gambling to speculating, hedging, trading, and investing,

▶ the vast amounts of types of contracts that can be written and the multitude of ways they can be executed,

▶ convincing us that the market provides economic value to consumers,

▶ convincing us that prices are discovered or reflected, not created,

▶ creating new games to generate additional revenue streams,

▶ creating a problem that didn't exist (volatility),

▶ creating hedging to solve the problem (volatility) they created.

Don't count on the regulatory commissions to protect you as a *player*. As I discussed earlier, the job of a self-regulatory organization is to enforce minimum financial sales practice requirements for its members. Nowhere does it mention the *player*.

The true purpose of the regulatory agencies are to:
► make sure the exchanges are successful,
► make sure the winners get their $,
► make sure the losers can't hold the brokers or exchanges liable,
► make sure the brokers and exchanges are not required to keep any records negative to their success.

I want to show you that if you study the commodity markets, they will tell you everything you need to know.

As one of the three regulatory agencies of the commodity market, (the other two being the Commodities Futures Trading Commission (CFTC) and the Futures Commissions Merchants (FCM)), the National Futures Association (NFA) regulates every firm or individual who conducts futures trading business with public customers.

If you contact the NFA and tell them you are interested in the commodities market, they will send you a booklet, entitled *"Opportunities and Risk: An Educational Guide to Trading Futures and Options on Futures."* The booklet will tell you this about the commodities market:
► It's very risky
► It's very volatile
► Only use risk capital *you can afford to lose* [italics mine]

Brokers who successfully promote the commodities market are one part master salesman and one part con-man. The master salesman attracts your participation. From that point on, he leads you to believe that if you play the game right, using all his "expert" (but non-binding) advice, you will win. These are classic elements of a con game.

The booklet points out that success is based primarily on a *player's* emotional makeup; that many people are not "mentally qualified to trade." If you follow the advice and lose your $, you are prepared to accept their escape: It wasn't their fault you lost your $. You weren't "mentally qualified to trade."

"Opportunity and Risk"
I'm going to show you one example of how the NFA uses illusion and deception to give you a false sense of security. Below, you see the front cover of the booklet published by the NFA, called "Opportunity and Risk: An Educational Guide to Trading Futures and Options on Futures":

There is an illustration of a tightrope with one person on it, and one safely across. The man on the tightrope looks stable with an umbrella for balance, and has an excellent chance of making it across. The cover implies that, although there is a risk of falling, investors can make it safely across.

This is deceiving and in no way accurately describes the risks of the commodity markets. The illusion is that, despite the risk, there is always a positive outcome. They use the title "Opportunity and Risk," as though they are equal, but they fail to provide any statistics to give us any sense of what is more likely to happen.

If the illustration were accurate, here's how the cover should look:

Opportunity (5%) and Risk (95%)

In the bottom of the "pit," there should be a large collection of bodies of those who didn't make it across the tightrope as well as people continually falling into the pit. And the person on the rope doesn't look secure or stable at all. Now, while this may not be the marketing pitch the NFA wants to send out, this is a more accurate way of presenting the risks involved in playing the commodities markets.

The NFA mission statement
When you open the booklet, you are provided the NFA mission statement on page two: *"National Futures Association is a congressionally authorized self-regulated organization of the United States futures industry. Its mission is to provide innovative regulatory programs and services that protect investors and ensure market integrity."* [Italics mine]

Interesting. Let's look at that simple mission statement in more detail. They have been legally authorized by the government to regulate the commodity markets. With that in mind, if you remember my definition of a self-regulated organization, then you know that they:

▶ create rules and regulations to ensure the success of the organization,
▶ make sure the winners get their $,
▶ make sure the losers can't hold the brokers and exchanges liable,
▶ not require any records be published that are negative to the success of the organization.

Therefore from the very beginning you are told that the NFA is a self-regulated organization, and if the commodity markets no longer existed, they would be out of a job. So, as long as everyone plays by the rules, the job of the NFA is to protect the markets from the *players* and not the *players* from the markets.

As I've said before, the fox is in charge of the hen house.

The NFA promotes their "innovative regulatory programs" as exciting new ways to invest in commodities. They tout tightly controlled rules. All of this, they say, is designed in the *players'* best interest. Of course, it's all an illusion.

In fact, these "innovative regulatory programs" consist of a whole host of highly complex games in order to ensure a steady flood of losers with regulations to protect the brokers and exchanges from liability from the losers. It's the losers, not the winners, who keep the markets operating.

You are conditioned to believe that when the regulatory commissions create rules to "protect the investors," they are protecting the *players* from losing their $

Crazyman $ays:
"It's the information they
don't provide that is
the most important."

from bad advice from brokers or financial advisors. The *players* are, in fact, protected from anyone breaking the rules. But the rules are written to protect the exchanges from the *players*, not to protect the losers from the exchanges. Nothing is written about how a loser can get their $ back when everyone plays by the rules. The losers support the winners, and the losers have no legal recourse. So how can that work in the best interests of the *players*?

"Market integrity" is another interesting term here. It gives you the impression that the markets are a fair place to do business. But the rules are written to protect the exchanges, and the only thing the *player* is protected against is anyone breaking the rules. This is far from "fair," since 95 percent of *players* lose $ in the markets. The NFA doesn't publish the fact that *players* are participating in a minus-sum game, or that the markets depend on the losers to survive.

The NFA does ensure that everyone plays by the rules, and brokers will talk about how tough these rules are. But they are primarily designed to collect margin $ to guarantee that the winners get their $. This way, the markets can claim "market integrity," brokers can brag about following the rules, and the *player* has a false sense of security that their best interests are being taken care of.

What the NFA booklet tells you...
The NFA booklet is full of general quotes about their function that have no factual basis. For example, on page six of the booklet, you see the following:

"For nearly a century and a half, markets have fulfilled an important economic function: providing an efficient and effective mechanism for the management of price risks."

This is simply not true, as it is neither efficient nor effective. When you look at the billions of dollars that are in motion every day in the market, with the prices constantly changing, how is that efficient? If a majority of people are buying and selling contracts, and a majority of contracts purchased are not delivered, how is this process beneficial for anyone but the Fat Cats?

Weak words
Both the NFA and the financial industry in general are infamous for phrasing vague concepts. A "built-in disclaimer" is created to avoid commitment to any statement.

If you read the NFA booklet, you will see the following weak words used continually:

▶ Can

▶ Should/should not

▶ Possibility

▶ Possibly

▶ Potentially

▶ In light of

▶ In part

▶ May/may be

Here's a typical sentence on page eight of the booklet which describes the steadfast confidence that the NFA has in you playing the commodity markets:

Margin $ - Down
payment the holder of a
contract uses to cover
the risk.

"For *those individuals* who *fully
understand* and *can* afford the risks
which are involved, the allocation of
some portion of their capital to futures
trading can provide a means of achieving
greater diversification and a *potentially*
higher overall rate of return on their
investments." [Italics mine]

In fact, when you read the whole booklet,
you can't find anything that is concrete.
This isn't isolated to the NFA booklet.
Just read or watch any financial services
commercial and see if you can spot all of
the weak words. By using these weak
words, they are giving the reader an
illusion of commitment. From my
perspective, here's the difference:

You will win a million dollars.
You **can** win a million dollars.

Which one locks me into a commitment?
Using weak words prevents them from
being locked in to any statement, and
you can't legally depend on or draw a
conclusion from the statement. This
allows the NFA to avoid actual
accountability and responsibility. And it
shifts the blame solely to the *player*.

The NFA booklet also describes how
players provide "an active liquid and
competitive market." What this means is
that a liquid market ensures that there
are sufficient contracts outstanding and
adequate buyers and sellers to have
enough $ to cover large transactions
without a substantial change in price.

The liquidity of the market comes from
the margin $ held in escrow and the
number of people holding contracts. This
margin $ will guarantee that the winners
get their $.

Today, with far less than one percent of all futures contracts dealing with actual commodities, it didn't take long for the markets to realize how they could receive additional $ from *players*. When market exchanges required both sellers and buyers to make a margin deposit they realized that much of this $ would remain in their possession for days and weeks. Exchanges do not pay any interest on margin $ they collect from *players* creating an additional source of revenue at *players'* expense. To put this into perspective, consider this: As of March 1, 2008, the New York Mercantile Exchange told me on the phone that they had $25 BILLION of margin $ on hand. Now, at five percent interest, that is $1.25 billion generated before the doors even open. On the same day, the Chicago Board of Trade told me they had $2 billion on hand in margin $ for just corn futures.

Just on the interest alone, the markets ensure their continuing success.

Price management

The NFA claims the commodities market uses price management to maintain a fair pricing of all commodities on the market. And this price management is beneficial to consumers by providing a strong economic function by keeping prices low. This is simply not true.

The markets become a plus to the producer and a negative to the consumer. Markets are restricted in the way they set prices by the parameters of what they call a "reasonable profit" and pricing it out of the market. This allows the producers to work from a baseline of reasonable profit and up. If the markets set prices too low, then the producers will remove it from trading. The price has to stop going up when it prices the product out of the market. This is the parameter within which the markets work. Thus, when the consumer is charged a price above "reasonable profit," the consumer pays more because it means the producers have used the markets in their advantage to price their products above what they could normally charge.

In addition, a company that has products represented in the commodity markets can charge higher prices and use the commodity markets as a scapegoat. How? One of the first things you need to know is that a producer doesn't have to use the market price. They can sell it at any price they want. But when the commodity markets drive the price up, the producers as a whole can use the markets to their advantage to gouge the consumer and avoid prosecution for price fixing because they are using "market price." They are able to manipulate the process in their best interest of higher profits instead of that of the consumer.

I have no problem with companies making a profit. Just don't tell me that this is in the best interest of keeping consumer prices low. That is a falsehood. Why wouldn't a producer be involved in the commodity markets when they can get "reasonable profit" and above for their products? Any producer will not produce a product for long when they are losing $. They use the commodities market to create higher profits for themselves, blame the market process for the price increases, and the consumer pays higher prices.

Let's talk about gas prices. You've noticed that gas prices change daily or sometimes even a couple of times per day. There is no way this is a result of supply and demand, and it isn't a result of oil companies needing to raise prices to offset production costs to ensure they make a profit. Oil prices have to remain between "reasonable profit" and pricing the product out of the market. Our economy is very strongly petroleum-based, and due to that necessity, we are paying close to and over $100 barrel for oil (as of March, 2008) or over $3 for a gallon of gas. OPEC doesn't meet daily to determine supply and demand. That shows that the oil companies set prices without fear of prosecution and make record-profits.

I'm sure you don't know this, but producers are allowed to buy and sell commodity contracts of their own products thus having an unfair influence on market price. This is an outrageous conflict of interest. How can an oil company be fair, equitable, and working for the consumer when they can manipulate the price in their best interest? Congress needs to shut this barn door.

Reflect and price discovery
The commodity markets promote the fact that they manage price risk through reflecting and discovering prices, not by setting them. This is a very important difference since it removes any responsibility of high prices from the

producers and places it squarely on the market. But they claim that high prices are due to factors outside the control of the markets. This in and of itself is contradictory in nature. They claim this provides a very important economic function by keeping prices lower for the consumer. This is the key illusion and deception the MASTERS use.

I called the Chicago Board of Trade and found out how many contracts were sold in one commodity (corn) in January 2008, and how many were delivered.

Number of corn contracts sold:	4,213,195
Number of corn contracts delivered:	0

The consensus of all of these contracts sold is how they determined the price of corn. This was how much motion and revenue was created in one month on one commodity. The fees and commissions on this motion are in the hundreds of millions of dollars. The margin $ on hand for corn alone is almost $2 BILLION, which sits in escrow at the Chicago Board of Trade and earns interest, yet, no one can tell you how that margin $ is divided up.

I also contacted the New York Mercantile Exchange, and they gave me the following information about crude oil:

Number of crude oil contracts sold in January, 2008	10,814,818
Number of crude oil contracts delivered in January, 2008	0
Number of open-ended contracts	1,392,370

The consensus of all of these contracts sold is how they determined the price of crude oil, which consequently affects the gas prices you pay at the pump. This was how much motion and revenue was created in one month on one commodity. The fees and commissions on this motion are in the hundreds of millions of dollars. The NYME also revealed that they do not make public the amount of margin $ on hand for crude oil, but as a whole exchange, they have about $25 billion on escrow collecting interest.

In the NFA booklet, when discussing price discovery, this is what they tell you:

"As the term indicates, futures markets 'discover'—or reflect—cash market prices. *They do not set them.*" [Italics mine]

Now, logic would suggest that the term "Reflect" would indicate that the price is already there to begin with. The term "Discover" would mean the price is already there. However, according to the NFA:

Price Discovery –
is the determination of a price by a market process.

Reflect –
The consensus of buyers and sellers opinions at that time.

So, by their own definition, prices are created through the consensus of the buyers and sellers. This is inconsistent with their claims that prices are discovered.

Listen, the fact is The New York Mercantile Exchange does not call every gas station in the country every morning and ask them what their gas prices are in order to determine prices for oil contracts. Contracts are bought and sold based solely on individual contracts being sold with the intent to resell that contract at a profit. As a result, prices are set by the buyers and sellers of the contracts, not on supply and demand. OPEC does not meet daily to determine gas prices, and prices are not determined on current supply and demand.

The reason prices continually change is simple: In order for the exchanges to stay in business, the prices have to constantly change in order to create motion, which results in fees and commissions for the exchanges and brokers. The NFA even acknowledges that in the booklet:

"The process of reassessment (price discovery) is continuous."
(NFA – page 20)
And,
"...The only certainty is that the price will change."
(NFA – Page 21)

Myriad factors
Hopefully, by now, you understand how the commodity markets deceive the public by trying to convince us that prices are created primarily through supply and demand. In fact, prices that the mercantile exchanges establish are determined through the consensus of the buyers and sellers of the contracts. But if you read carefully, the NFA contradicts any possibility that supply and demand can be how prices are discovered. How? They use the term "myriad factors" to explain how prices increase and decrease through a wide variety of

causes completely outside the control of the markets. This is important, since "myriad" is defined as *"an indefinitely great number."*

When you hear on the news that commodities prices rose or fell due to supply and demand, or by an act of nature, the actual fact is that there are an infinite number of factors *players* use to determine market prices.

Let's review:
- ▶ Prices are "set" through the consensus of the buyers and sellers based on a myriad of factors.
- ▶ The markets do not "reflect" or "discover" cash market prices.
- ▶ Prices are created through individual players' mental process using an infinite number of factors to outguess another *player* in predicting an unpredictable to make $.
- ▶ Players rely on their emotions and ego to establish a price instead of any scientific or mathematical formula.

Onions and diamonds

Sounds like two contradictory items (although I guess both can make women cry). So, why am I bringing these up? Well, in 1958, Congress removed futures trading for onions. And what happened since? In the 50 years since, onions have continued being harvested and sold. There has not been any report of an onion shortage, nor have there been any reports that onion prices have been subject to excessive price increases in comparison to other commodities. The same can be said for tenderloins as well as any number of products not on the futures market. The prices of onions remain constant and reasonable, their availability remains strong, and this was done without the "help" of the commodity markets.

What about diamonds? In this case, as
of January 2008, the price of gold
approached $900/ounce for the first time.
But what about the price of diamonds?
Since they're not listed on the exchange,
you'd have to check with your local
jeweler. I would imagine that diamond
prices have remained fairly consistent
over the years and remain an important
investment to a certain segment of
the population.

It is argued that there is no futures
market for diamonds because of the
variations that exist from diamond to
diamond. The real commodity, they
claim, is carbon. However, the
fundamental value of the carbon in a
diamond is quite trivial. It is only when
the carbon in a diamond is configured in
a very specific way that the diamond
then has value.

The diamond markets and onion markets
have managed price risks all by
themselves without any help, and both
industries still appear to be thriving. The
fact that some commodities are left off
proves the markets can't claim to provide
an important economic function if all
products are not represented.

Price Risk
Management of Price Risk – Speculators
seek the price risk that hedgers seek
to avoid.

Commodities markets always talk about
risks. This is another brilliant move by
the MASTERS.

By talking about risks:
▶ The reward in business is payment
    for taking risks.
▶ The MASTERS shift risk from one
    party to another.

▶ This shifting motion increases costs
to our society.
▶ The reason is the cost of insurance is
passed along to the consumer.
▶ Risk is what business is all about.
▶ The MASTERS are playing on our
instincts to seek financial security.
▶ In our search for security, we are
vulnerable to the MASTERS plan to
avoid risk.

This transfer of risk generates another
revenue stream by creating motion
where none existed before. In the final
analysis, you don't avoid risk, you just
pay to shift it from party to another.
And that cost is passed along to
the consumer.

At the end of the day, the NFA booklet
fails to reveal any statistics about the
true risks of the commodity markets and
takes advantage of weak words to give
you a false sense of security. If you read
all 93 pages, you will notice that it fails to
mention the exact number of *players* that
lose $, or how much, or how the margin
$ is divided up. In fact, you will be hard-
pressed to find any real statistics at all.
They never give you any percentages of
failure or success. They never give you
any percentage of winners to losers or
the percentage of people who win $ on
specific commodities.

If the NFA was serious about protecting
players, they would demand full
disclosure from exchanges of the
following:
▶ how many *players* lost $ and how
much;
▶ the brokers' honest account of the $
lost by all of their *players*;

▶ the amount of $ that *players* spent on fees, commissions and taxes;

▶ and how this impacted the *players'* overall performance.

Then *players* as a whole would realize that they are not investing They are gambling, playing games of chance with the odds firmly stacked against them.

This is why brokers won't give you a performance report, and that's why the commissions don't require such documents. To do so would be to expose the corridor to their success. Brokers who ballyhoo the success of their clients are blowing wind into the sail of a sinking boat.

Chapter Seven:
— Hedging, derivatives and degree days —

I tried to make sure this book didn't get so complex you would lose the message, but I needed to mention hedging, derivatives, and degree days. These are some of the MASTERS most brilliant pieces of work. Like all illusions and deceptions, they seem complex. However, when exposed, they are simple ways to bring new *players* into a game.

Hedging replaces speculating under the illusion of solving a problem that the MASTERS created. The problem that was created by the MASTERS was volatility in the markets. This volatility was created by constantly changing prices. The market has now created an environment where the producers of a commodity believe they have to protect themselves from this volatility. What draws the producer (a *player* who produces a commodity) into the system is his search for security and his belief that the system will insure him against constantly adverse changing prices.

The MASTERS have offered a solution to this insecurity to avoid adverse price

Crazyman $ays:
"Hedging is a market creation to convince producers that speculating has a positive outcome by providing insurance against adverse price changes."

Producer – Someone who actually is in charge of bringing the commodity (corn, oil, grain, etc.) to market. Farmers are the most well-known producers, but it could be other providers as well.

Contract market – The buying and selling of commodity contracts without the need for delivery of the product.

Cash market – Bringing your commodity to the market to sell for cash.

changes and called it hedging. If the producer of a commodity gets more $ out of the commodity contract than his cash crop would have brought, then he considers himself a winner. If he loses $, they convince him that he did not lose; he just covered (offset) his losses with his cash crop. At this point, he feels satisfied that he has insured his product against adverse price changes.

In fact, the MASTERS have now pulled him into a minus-sum game in which he will lose $ on 95 percent of his contracts. The producer is gambling by participating in a solution, called "hedging," to a problem that the markets themselves created. And since the producer is largely unaware of the web of illusion and deception he's been drawn into, the process keeps going on. Every contract he purchases creates motion, which takes $ out of his pocket and puts $ in the pockets of Fat Cats.

When you buy a commodity contract, you are a *player*, period. That's as simple as it gets. To be able to keep from getting confused, you've got to understand that when you purchase a contract, it is a completely separate function than selling a product on a cash market. No matter how you look at it, when you buy and sell a contract, you will either make $ or lose $. And when you sell your product on the cash market, you will either make $ or lose $. The only connection between a corn contract and a corn producer is the use of the word "corn." You don't have to be a corn producer to buy a corn contract. Again, they are two separate entities mutually exclusive of each other. The brilliance of the plan is how they tied them together.

The MASTERS convinced producers that if they lose $ in the commodities market, they didn't really lose it, they offset it with their cash crop. What this means is that they've convinced the producers to gamble by purchasing on a contract, and if they lose $, then the $ brought in will make up for the $ lost on the contract. In actuality, their cash crop brought the price the market offered, and the contract was bought and sold separately. The producers believe they broke even, when in fact, they have lost $.

By falling into this illusion, producers are led to believe that cash contracts and commodities contracts are intertwined. They are deceived into believing that by offsetting, they can protect against losses on their cash crop. They are tricked into participating in gambling games and calling it insurance. The reality is that markets don't care where you get the $ to pay them. The gambler that lost $ on his corn contract knows he lost $. The producer that loses $ on his corn contract believes that the price for his corn crop offsets his losses. In both cases, there is a negative $ for the *players*. With two similar, but separate, entities intertwined, producers are seduced into participating. MASTERS have deployed a brilliant marketing strategy.

Crazyman $ays:
"Gamblers don't count their losses, they only count their winnings."

What draws players to the game?
Constantly changing prices and buying and selling by the second are the main ingredients of the commodities market. A producer is lured in by his search for financial security and is tempted by the prospects of taking a little $ and turning it into a lot of $ quickly without effort.

These prices are always changing due to the buyers and sellers based on an infinite (myriad) amount of factors including the judgment and emotions of the *players*. This volatility keeps *players'* $ in motion. And the market itself creates the volatility which results in constantly changing prices. By keeping them guessing about the changing prices, producers and *players* alike are drawn in by using factors other than supply and demand.

As a reminder: This is how a producer/player can possibly, but not probably turn their $ quickly in the stock market:

If you plug any number into the equation and do the math, you can see the appeal.

Pyramid of wealth formula

The percentage gained

x the number of trades per day x 365 days

1% gain x 10 trades per day

10% return per day x

365 days

= 3,650%.

Margins are an added lure to bring *players* to the tables. They have no use other than to draw the *players* in to a pure gambling scenario. A margin is a portion paid of true value which in the commodities markets comes out to approximately 1/20th.

By putting up 1/20th of the value of a commodity, *players* can make 20 times return of its true value. This allows *players* to turn a little $ into a lot of $ quickly without effort.

Now, I'll show you the same formula using margin $:

Margins also make it possible to sell the contract and buy back more than you sold with the same $. For example, if corn is $2.00 and margins are 1/20th, you pay 10 cents in margin $ to buy a bushel of corn ($2.00/20+10 cents). If corn goes up 10 cents, you can sell it for 20 cents and take the 20 cents and buy two bushels of corn for the initial investment of 10 cents.

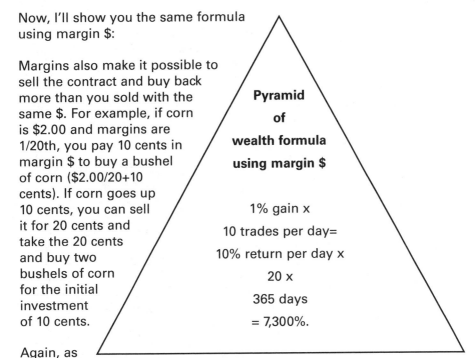

Pyramid

of

wealth formula

using margin $

1% gain x

10 trades per day=

10% return per day x

20 x

365 days

= 7,300%.

Again, as I mentioned earlier, this potential to continually double your money, despite the risks, is what draws *players* into the game.

In creating "hedging," the brilliance of the MASTERS is that they:
▶ changed "speculating" into "hedging;"
▶ created a problem that didn't exist;
▶ created a solution to the problem they created;
▶ convinced producers that they weren't gambling, they were insuring your product;
▶ allowed producers to use margin $ in hopes of turning a little $ into a lot of $ quickly;
▶ turned the negative performance of speculating into an illusion of a positive outcome of hedging for the producer.

You have to admit, this is pretty
ingenious on the part of the MASTERS.
They're teaching you that you're insuring
a positive with a negative. And the
truth is producers will not produce a
product for long losing $. The process is
positive to the producer and negative to
the consumer.

So, why do you need the markets?

Derivatives

The MASTERS took advantage of our
search for security and figured out that
some people are willing to bet on
anything. The commodity markets took
advantage and expanded their games to
allow *players* to risk their $ on an array
of intangibles and insignificant events.

This allowed the commodities market to
expand from corn and oil to non-tangible
items such as degree days and cell
phone minutes. The exchanges call these
derivatives. Derivatives are the most
transparent example of gambling in its
purist form. By introducing derivatives,
the number of items on which to buy and
sell contracts has expanded
tremendously, as well as the number of
players willing to risk their $ on these
new games. As a result, there were over
$516 Trillion in derivatives contracts in
circulation in March, 2008, according to
the most recent survey by the Bank of
International Settlements, the world's
clearinghouse for central banks in Basel,
Switzerland. The fact is that this is all
perceived value. There's no $ there.

An entire book can be written on
derivatives. That experts in the financial
field have trouble properly defining what

derivatives are and how they work
proves that the MASTERS got it right. I
define a derivative as anything that can
be assigned a value that has a perceived
effect on someone's profit or loss.

The characteristics of derivatives:
▶ It's an extension or evolution of the
   MASTERS to keep $ in motion by
   creating an almost unlimited amount
   of new revenue streams;
▶ This creates a perceived value with
   no $ to back it up;
▶ Under false pretenses, it has an
   economic value;
▶ It is a minus-sum game to *players*;
▶ The more motion that is created, the
   less $ *players* have, and the more $
   Fat Cats accumulate without
   producing anything of value;
▶ This creates an unstable economic
   environment;
▶ If the government can't understand it,
   they can't regulate it, so then they
   need to do away with it.

The brilliance of their plan is that by
using intangibles, they have been able to
sell the concept that derivatives are
another way to hedge risk.

Honestly, derivatives are nothing more
than gambling games, just another way
to separate $ from the masses and
placing it in motion. Almost anything can
be used as a point of reference for
purchasing a contract to try and outguess
another *player*. At the end of the day,
derivatives contribute no more economic
value to the country than playing Texas
hold-em poker provides an economic
value to Texas.

Derivatives are basically a casino on
steroids where securities which have no

Here's a partial list:

Clean Air Degree Days Index, Atlanta

Degree Days Index, Boston

Degree Days Index, Chicago

Degree Days Index, Cincinnati

Degree Days Index, Dallas

Degree Days Index,
Des Moines

Degree Days Index,
Kansas City

Degree Days Index,
Las Vegas

Degree Days Index, Minneapolis

Degree Days Index,
New York

Degree Days Index, Philadelphia

Degree Days Index,
Portland

Degree Days Index, Tucson

Seasonal Degree
Days Index

Atlanta Seasonal
Degree Days Index

Seasonal Degree Days Index, Las Vegas

Pacific Rim Index, Osaka

Seasonal, Pacific Rim Index Tokyo

Heating Degree Days, Amsterdam

Seasonal Heating Degree Days, Berlin

Monthly Heating Degree Days, Berlin

Seasonal Heating Degree Days, London

Monthly Heating Degree Days, Paris

Monthly Heating Degree Days, Paris

Seasonal Heating Degree Days, Stockholm

Monthly Heating Degree Days

Seasonal Temperature Cumulative Average, Stockholm

intrinsic value but which represent bets on other securities are traded for ridiculously high paper profit. When that house of cards falls, it will likely take much of the larger economy with it. Pension funds, banks, brokerages, and other institutions holding worthless hedge fund paper are forced under by tremendous losses.

Degree days
To the left is another outrageous example of what *players* can bet on in the commodities markets. We know playing the commodities market can involve everything from traditional examples like oil and corn to newer games like cell minutes and band-width. An absurd concept, offering the buying of futures contracts based on various weather related events, is highly popular in commodity markets.

What in the world are *players* betting on when they take a position on these various weather futures contracts?

The MASTERS have created an almost unlimited way for *players* to hand over their $ and made it so complex as to keep them involved. Each level of complexity and each new game brings in new *players* and creates motion. Believe me, if you look at the number of combinations of shares or contracts you can purchase, this is just the tip of the iceberg.

Chapter Eight:
— The brilliance of the MASTERS —

There's a gentleman named "John" (not his real name) I speak to frequently when I'm having lunch at the diner in Veedersburg. He took an early retirement from GM and decided to take the advice of a broker and invest his retirement $. He lost a substantial amount in the market due to this trust. The amazing

thing is that he blames himself for his losses. Time after time I've explained to him how he was conned out of his retirement, and he tells me it's his own fault.

The sad thing is that all across the country there are people like John who were conned out of their money but too proud or embarrassed to do anything about it. The fact that the MASTERS know this and exploit this is a travesty.

Crazyman $ays:
"The brilliance of the MASTERS is that when you lose $ by following their system, they'll convince you it's your fault."

By now you've realized that you are a *player*, participating in a con designed to separate you from your $. But who is responsible for setting this system up and keeping it going? To understand how you have been conditioned and manipulated over the years, you have to understand how this was put into place.

There are five basic ways to acquire money:

1. Profit from producing a product
2. Providing a service
3. Gift-Given to you
4. Stealing it
5. **Manipulating** it

The MASTERS have set up an entire system based on manipulating $ from the masses without producing any goods or services. As I said in the introduction, entire books can be written about various individuals who helped put this system into place. If the system works to your advantage, you're going to work hard to keep it in place. You would train your successor to keep it going in their time. That's why it's not important to get caught up in individual names, because they're just people who made it to the top of their field and found out that they had to work hard to keep the $ rolling in. In their quest, this group has spent generations studying and understanding human behavior. As a result, they perfected a system to con the masses out of their $ without question, prosecution, or accountability. They are Masters of Illusion and Deception.

Over time they developed such a complex system that the masses do not understand it; the media and academic world promotes it; the government cannot control or regulate it properly. Therefore, the MASTERS keep perpetuating their con game, and it continues to get bigger and bigger while trying to satisfy their addiction to wealth at *players'* expense.

I have to give them credit. I'm extremely impressed with their abilities. This process did not happen overnight. It began with the conception of markets and has evolved and developed over the course of generations. The MASTERS have developed an incredibly sophisticated and confusing system to keep the con going. How is it that they conned us out of billions of dollars a day without question? They've convinced us to believe that, by following their system, you can turn a little $ into a lot of $ without effort.

How did they implement their system to pursue greed without remorse?

1. They had to change your mindset from the idea of playing gambling games to performing a very vital economic function by investing your $.
2. They created a system that was so complex; the news media supports it; the academic world teaches it; elected officials have legalized it; and the masses believe in it unquestionably and without demand for accountability.
3. They convinced regulatory agencies to make rules so complicated that only a select few can understand it.
4. They designed it so no one would ask for a performance report from brokers and exchanges, and the government wouldn't require it.
5. They created a system in which no one knows, questions, or appears to care where their winnings come from.
6. They deceived us into believing the terms "published value," "perceived value," and "outperformed"

represented real value. They are words of illusion and deception.

7. They created a problem that didn't exist and offered "hedging" as a solution to the problem.
8. They created such a complex web that even if one part is damaged or removed, another quickly replaces it.
9. They promoted the market as being an essential part of the economy to the point that anyone who challenges the system is "anti-American" or "anti-capitalism."
10. They created the ultimate con by convincing us it's our fault we lose $ by playing their con games.

The brilliance of the ultimate con is that, like John, you take responsibility for your losses. You don't seek retribution from the brokers or demand that our elected officials step in on your behalf.

The MASTERS' use of psychology and behavioral finance

If I were to run a gambling organization, the most important thing I would do is take a course in human behavior. The casinos, markets, and exchanges knew this early on and have become experts in understanding psychology to separate *players* from their $ without question.

The MASTERS have spent untold amounts of $ researching human behavior and perfected ways to take advantage of every human weakness to separate the masses from their $. They have spent years studying and applying the science of human nature to convince you to trust them by convincing you it's "investing." Why do they spend so much time on studying psychology?

The answer is simple: Wall Street alone controls approximately 8.4 trillion dollars of your $. For every one percent they can skim off the top through fees and commissions, they stick another $84 billion in their pockets. Derivatives in the commodity markets account for $300 trillion. One percent off the top is $3 trillion. Approximately $2 billion in commodity contracts are traded per day. Do the math; count your $.

The MASTERS research uncovered that playing the markets, like gambling, is based on irrational behavior. We make decisions based on emotion rather than logic or information. This makes your minds easy to manipulate because the MASTERS tap into our desire for financial wealth and security. And this conditioning through illusion and deception has gone on for decades. Now, they have they started using new psychological technologies of what they called "behavioral finance." The MASTERS discovered that people are excited to be in on the latest system, and they've developed programs to use your enthusiasm against you. Again, all of the money spent is a drop in the bucket compared to what they can earn by keeping your $ in motion. Trust me, they are not working in your best interests.

Like any good ad campaign developed on Madison Avenue, every investment ad you see or sales pitch you hear is a result of proven psychological and marketing tricks developed by the MASTERS. In order to get their hands on your $, they use proven visuals and spokesmen to convince you that you are not gambling and are not taking an unacceptable risk.

Crazyman $ays:
"The MASTERS don't
share the good deals, they
market the bad ones."

Remember, it makes no difference to them if you win $ or lose $, only that you keep your $ in motion.

The MASTERS play with *players'* minds on two levels: novice *players* are convinced that investing is "safe." Your insecurities are intensified when you are convinced that, if you're smart and listen to the right people, you can accumulate wealth quickly. (And oh, by the way, it will be mentioned in passing that you can lose all of your $. However, if you listen to their advice, that won't happen to you.)

So, let's be clear, the MASTERS use tricks of Vegas, Madison Avenue, and psychologists to engage in a psychological war on the minds of average Americans trying to hold on to their retirement savings.

How the MASTERS use the three C's, Camouflage, Conditioning, and Convincing to separate *players* from their $:
► They created an illusion and deception to camouflage risk so *players* will believe their $ is safe;
► They condition *players* to believe that stocks and commodities are vital to the economy;
► They convince *players* that they are only looking after their best interests.

They do this by changing your mindset from gambling to investing, speculating, hedging, and trading. But one thing is for certain—you are their prey.

The objective of the MASTERS is to create a dependent *player*, not an informed *player*. Remember, they don't care if you win or lose, only that you continue to play. They only care about keeping *players'* $ in motion. They know *players* as a whole are poorly educated about how to play the markets. They also know most *players* are insecure, vulnerable, and often irrational. The MASTERS know *players* are easy to deceive, manipulate, and control. The *player* wants to "win big," and the MASTERS consistently exploit that desire to separate these innocents from their $.

The MASTERS can keep the academic world working with them by generously awarding consulting contracts, grants and retainers to hire the best talent in investment psychology (yes, there is such a thing) to work on perfecting the con to manipulate you. That guarantees the MASTERS will achieve their target not only of developing dependent *players*, but they will bait the new blood needed to keep the markets going.

Don't believe me? Take a moment and look up the Nobel Prize® winner for Economics in 2002. You may be surprised to discover that it was awarded to Daniel Kahneman, a psychologist, not an economist.

The MASTERS set up a system that benefited those who kept the status quo in place.

Owning a seat on the exchange gives you special advantages
When you are a *player* in the stock market, you rely on the information you have either researched yourself or have received from a broker or $ manager. Both ways will provide you with outdated information the moment it hits your

hand. Receiving current information is not possible as you are not legally allowed access to inside information. When stock information finally trickles down to you, the party's been over for about six months.

Yet, there are those who will purchase a seat on the New York Stock Exchange for as high as four million dollars. Common logic would suggest that spending millions of dollars to get access to a seat on any exchange provides enormous advantages that are worth the $ spent.

Owning a seat on the NYSE enables one to trade on the floor of the exchange, as an agent either for someone else (floor broker) or for one's own personal account(floor trader).

What do these people get in return for this seat?
1. Immediate access to information an average *player* doesn't have which results in instant decisions profitable to the seat owner.
2. They also do not have to pay fees, resulting in larger profit margins than average *players*.
3. They collect fees from other *players*.
4. The ability to move swiftly on slight changes in price.

The price paid for a seat on the NYSE gives the owner substantial advantages. They have instant access to information to benefit them immediately. This instant access to information may only gain brokers an advantage as small as pennies per stock, but by buying huge amounts without having to pay fees, they benefit by millions of dollars.

Average *players* are at a substantial
disadvantage. They are making
calculations with nothing more than
outdated information. *Players* have to
pay fees and commissions on each
movement. The playing field just gets
more and more slanted.

It's important to remember two things:
(1) these examples are only part of the
multitude of advantages Fat Cats use to
work the system in their favor (2) as we
associate playing the markets with the
gambling, we see these advantages
ensure that the average *player* is always
running as hard as he can with no hope
of catching up.

It's bad enough that *players* are
automatically engaged in a minus-sum
game, but the system allows for the
powerful and influential to have added
advantages. If Congress demanded full
disclosure and accountability, more
pressure would be placed on the
exchanges and corporate boards to end
these unfair practices.

The role of the media as part of the MASTERS

Whatever your views on the media,
whether you think there is a "left-wing
bias" or a "vast right-wing conspiracy,"
you need to believe one thing: The media
is fully in the pocket of the MASTERS
and the Fat Cats on Wall Street. I don't
think it's evil as much as simple
economics and ignorance. The media's
livelihood depends on ratings,
readership, ad revenue, and good will
from a strong financial market. Positive
coverage gets more access to the Fat
Cats. Plus, they continue getting invited

to all the best parties. As I've said, the system is so complex, that the "talking heads" who cover the markets are reading the same cue cards as your local newscaster.

National media's promotion of a healthy market is in their own best self-interest. You are relentlessly battered with information about the markets: stock market updates on the radio and television, business section of the local paper, cable channels devoted solely to daily coverage of every bit of news related primarily to New York Stock Exchange, NASDAQ, the Chicago Board of Trade, and the New York Mercantile Exchange. It's enough to boggle the most discerning mind.

If you read any ad, profile or story about the stock market or a financial planner, you'll notice there is a rhythm to the story. The cadence leads readers along a path covering the risks and past the disclaimers to get to a place they want them to go. At the end, you're led to their web by their use of weak words, disclaimers and statements instead of statistics. They can claim "honesty" in their "hard-hitting" story while you dismiss the risk and focus on your Eagle's Eye view on what you've been conditioned to believe.

The funny thing is I believe the majority of the media types who cover Wall Street have no idea of the true nature of the markets. This blissful ignorance by media members of the markets ensure they keep their job while being an accomplice (willing or unwilling) of the MASTERS.

The end result is a persistent daily blitz
of news, 99 percent of which is
conditioning through exaggeration and
promotion, and one percent reality. The
news is spun by the MASTERS to
influence *players* to continue to hand
over their hard-earned $ and keep it
in motion.

The media just puts out the propaganda
that they are furnished. At no time does
the media publish how much $ *players*
have to lose every day to keep them all
in business.

In the eyes of the media when covering
the markets, there are no red states or
blue states, only green.

The absurdity and brain trickery of the Dow Jones and S&P 500

Every day, you read and hear about how
the Dow Jones Industrial Average (DJIA)
and Standard & Poor's (S&P 500® is
used in reference not only to the index
but also to the 500 actual companies, the
stocks of which are included in the index)
performed for the day with the
information sometimes leading the news.
It is hyped, promoted, obsessed over,
and followed passionately, but let me ask
you a question:

What *exactly* is the Dow Jones?

I could ask people on the street and very
few, if any, could give me an accurate
answer. The Dow Jones is a reporting
device consisting of 30 companies on the
NYSE out of more than 11,000 used to
estimate "trends" in the market. That is a
statistical average of 0.0027 percent of all
of the listed companies.

Yet, you hear about it daily, and cable channels, newspapers, and magazines are dedicated to following its every move. But what is not reported is how you are deceived into believing that the Dow Jones has any value to *players*. The simple fact is that it has no value.

The truth is that the Dow Jones is simply a tool the MASTERS promote as a motivating device to give *players* a statistical point of reference every day to work from. The fact that the daily numbers are meaningless is not reported by the media. The Dow Jones can add or remove companies at their discretion and to the benefit of their report.

Market experts will admit that the daily numbers are not important but to focus on "trends." Although you've been taught to believe, without question, that the Dow Jones is vitally important, there is no formula that shows how the Dow Jones can make you $. There are also no statistics available that show you that the Dow Jones has any value to *players*.

Every day we hear and read whether the markets are up or down. We hear about what or where "investors" are looking for that particular day. There is no definition ever given as to who these "investors" are. There is no explanation as to why opinions of the unnamed few are affecting the trends of the markets. Yet this doesn't prevent average Americans from getting concerned and making decisions based on the movement of the markets even though the companies reporting to Dow Jones have very little impact on their daily lives. The Dow Jones is the measurement of 0.0027 percent of listed companies and has no mathematical or scientific value in predicting a non-predictable or making $ for *players* as a whole.

The Dow Jones is just another tool in the complex plan developed by the MASTERS to create the illusion that it appears to have real value. Brokers use it to their advantage to show *players* a chart depicting the rise of the markets over the years. A false sense of security is created among new *players*, and that same fear keeps *players* already losing $.

If you look at any chart tracking the Dow Jones in the last 30 years, your first impression would be that the stock market has grown dramatically since 1980. Proponents of the markets will point to this chart as a positive. But the chart, like everything else the MASTERS promote, is incomplete. What the chart doesn't show you is the number of companies removed from the exchange or the number of *players* that won $ or lost $ during this time period. The MASTERS have convinced us that the stock market has grown 10 percent a year on average, when in fact, that is a manipulation of statistics.

Here's a simple example of how the MASTERS misuse statistics to convince us the stock market has grown 10 percent a year:

Let's say that in 1998, there are 100 listed companies	100
From 1998-2008 –	
They listed 220 new companies	+220
That should leave 320 listed companies, right?	**320**
What they don't tell you is from 1998-2008,	
120 companies were removed from trading	-120
This leaves 200 companies	200

The markets promote a 10% growth, but they don't promote the 120 companies that were removed from trading. Don't you wonder what happened to *players* who had shares of stock in the 120 companies that were de-listed?

What exactly is the S&P 500®?

The S&P 500® is a measuring device
used to track the trends of the top 500
publicly traded companies in the US. You
would think that these are the cream of
the crop. By investing in these high-end
companies, you would believe that it has
more added value than regular companies.
The fact is that when you buy stocks in a
S&P 500® company, you have entered
a minus-sum game. Your winnings come
from losing *players*, and your odds of
winning are not improved over any
other stock.

The risks involved in purchasing shares
in an S&P 500® company are the same
as any other stocks. You can't depend
on the S&P 500® because the 500 are
not consistent, and the values constantly
change. The $ a *player* makes is not
based on the performance of the
company, but if you've outguessed
other *players*. At the end of the day, the
players who purchased S&P 500® stocks
have less $ in their pocket than when
they started.

If the media were truly interested in
reporting on the markets, they would not
focus on meaningless indicators such as
the Dow Jones and S&P 500®. Instead,
they would report on the amount of $
individual *players* lose on any given day.

The Dow Jones and S&P 500® are
simply two of the myriad of factors used
in determining prices. The average
American doesn't know that the factors
that determine the Dow Jones are
constantly changing, and the companies
listed in the S&P 500® are constantly

changing. As a result, they have no real value; they are simply a statistical point of reference for reporting purposes.

On Wall Street, those clawing their way up the ladder are obsessed; addicted to wealth and power without remorse. They created a system which uses illusion and deception to bring in new *players* and persuade old *players* to keep playing. They've used the best psychological methods to camouflage the fact that you are gambling.

To perpetuate their power through the generations, the MASTERS have used their influence with politicians, lobbyists, SEC staffers, corporate CEO's, $ managers, reporters, brokers, and bankers. They have convinced them that the system is beneficial to all, and they have conditioned you to believe, without question, that *players* are not gambling and are not participating in a minus-sum game.

But the vast majority of *players* are passive prey targeted by aggressive parasites that pretend to be acting in the nation's best interests. The MASTERS hide behind many masks, as brokers, planners, investment advisors, financial consultants, or $ managers who are controlled by a system created by the MASTERS. It's a trap, and *players* are their victims.

Chapter Nine:

— Brokers—the face of the con —

There's a reason I don't mention any names of the MASTERS. It's because more than likely, you as a *player* will never come in contact with them. You'll never meet them, hear about them, or from them. They live and work in a world different than most of us will ever see. However, the brokers, the people who look you in the eye and tell you to trust them with your $, live and work in your town. They may have limited contact with the MASTERS as well, but they make a living based on the con set up by the MASTERS.

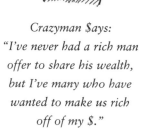

You may think that brokers are professional $ mangers working to keep you as a client by working in your best interest. The truth is their job is simply to make $ for themselves, their bosses and the exchanges. The key is that broker make more $ off of *players* that lose than *players* that win. Since the system survives on the losers, the job of the brokers is to consistently work to keep the *players* he has while recruiting new blood. The broker gets new *players* by focusing on the winners, and keeps *players* by concentrating on the losers. How can they do

Crazyman $ays:
"I've never had a rich man offer to share his wealth, but I've many who have wanted to make us rich off of my $."

that if 95 percent of people lose $? To do that, they need to mislead us.

When a broker is trained, they are taught proven and manipulative psychological tricks along with financial information. They may promote themselves as "investment advisors", but they are salesmen, first and foremost. As you might expect, a broker's so-called advice is self-serving and misleading. Anything they say and do enhances their efforts to close a sale. From their bosses they feel incessant pressure to perform. All the way from the top, it's rolling down. Their primary directive from their boss is to get clients $ in motion in order to generate commissions and fees.

In fact, the name "broker" has become such a dirty word that the MASTERS started using different terms. A "broker" became an "investment advisor" or "financial consultant," and they are there to provide "advice" to help *players* manage their $ not to sell you stocks or commodities contracts. And don't buy into the newest scam that brokers offer of no-fee services. What this means is that the fund managers are paying the commissions for bringing them clients, and believe me, the brokers know which ones are paying the highest commissions, and it has nothing to do with performance.

They convince you that they were working in your best interests when all they were doing was getting you to trust them to put your $ in motion, and then making $ off that motion. What this also does is allow brokers to utilize disclaimers and weak words to defend their position when you lose $.

Brokers and $ managers didn't tell you what to do with your $; they just gave you "advice." They didn't cause you to lose your $, they just "consulted" with you. If you lose $, it was because you didn't take the advice of the broker, or the markets acted in a way beyond what the broker expected. Ultimately, they blame your losses on your ignorance and ultimately on you.

How brokers mislead *players*:
► They use the Eagle's Eye view.
► They use weak words.
► They use words that have no value.
► They use misleading information.
► They use propaganda of company performance.
► They use the lack of, and manipulation of, statistics.
► They encourage "long-term" playing.
► They use lack of full disclosure and accountability.

The following four paragraphs are from John Allen Paulos' book *Innumeracy*. The Stock-Market Scam is a classic numbers game illustrating how players can be fooled into believing someone possesses predictive ability.

Some would-be advisor puts a logo on some fancy stationery and sends out 32,000 letters to potential investors in a stock letter. The letters tell of his company's elaborate computer model, his financial expertise and inside contacts. In 16,000 of these letters he predicts the index will rise, and in the other 16,000 he predicts a decline. No matter whether the index rises or falls, a follow-up letter is sent, but only to the 16,000 people who initially received the correct "prediction." To 8,000 of them, a rise is predicted for the next week; to the other 8,000, a decline. Whatever happens now, 8,000 people will have received two correct predictions. Again, to those 8,000 people only, letters are sent concerning the index's performance the following week: 4,000 predicting a rise; 4,000 a decline. Whatever the outcome, 4,000 people have now received three straight correct predictions.

This is iterated a few more times, until 500 people have received six straight correct "predictions." These 500 people are now reminded of this and told that in order to continue to receive this valuable information for the seventh week

continued

they must each contribute $500. If they all pay, that's $250,000 for our advisor. If this is done knowingly and with intent to defraud, this is an illegal con game. Yet it's considered acceptable if it's done unknowingly by earnest but ignorant publishers of stock newsletters, or by practitioners of quack medicine, or by television evangelists. There's always enough random success to justify almost anything to someone who wants to believe.

There is another quite different problem exemplified by these stock-market forecasts and fanciful explanations of success. Since they're quite varied in format and often incomparable and very numerous, people can't act on all of them. The people who try their luck and don't fare well will generally be quiet about their experiences. But there'll always be some people who will do extremely well, and they will loudly swear to the efficacy of whatever system they've used. Other people will soon follow suit, and a fad will be born and thrive for a while despite its baselessness.

There is a strong general tendency to filter out the bad and the failed and to focus on the good and the successful. Casinos encourage this tendency by making sure that every quarter that's won in a slot machine causes lights to blink and makes its own little tinkle in the metal tray. Seeing all the lights and hearing all the tinkles, it's not hard to get the impression that everyone's winning. Losses or failures are silent. The same applies to well-publicized stock market killings vs. relatively invisible stock market ruinations, and to the faith healer who takes credit for an accidental improvement but will deny responsibility if, for example, he ministers to a blind man who then becomes lame.

The scam analogy appears in numerous books with similar versions and appears relevant in many ways to *players*. Some books begin with sharing the information that many mutual fund companies offer numerous mutual funds. Did you ever consider that the more funds, or products, a company offers, the better the chances are that one of the funds will rank at the top of its category? The company can then focus its marketing efforts on those funds that have "outperformed" others while keeping quiet about the funds that underperformed. In succeeding periods, different funds will rise to outperform others with marketing efforts shifting to those funds, like a game of hop-scotch.

The manipulation of statistics
Here's an example of how an enterprising broker can manipulate statistics to convince you as a *player* that he has a way to beat the system as he tries to convince you to trust them with your $. Working from a theory he is perfecting, the broker calls 1000 *players* about his newest way to beat the system. He calls it "The Coin-Flip Method." The broker promises big returns to 500 of them if they take his expert advice and choose Mutual Fund A (aka "heads"). The other 500 he also promises big returns by following his expert advice and choosing Mutual Fund B (aka "tails"). "Tails" wins.

So the broker calls those 500 winners, promising 250 of them big returns if they follow his advice and chooses "heads," as a winner (and he was right on "tails") and the other 250 big returns by following his expert advice by choosing "tails" as a winner (and he was right on "tails"). The coin is flipped, and it's "heads," so the broker calls 250 *players*...and so on. For one lucky *player*, the broker is right 10 times in a row!

His success inspires the broker to publish a book called "The Coin Flip Method." In it he claims his system "produced 999 out of 1000 winners." But he hasn't given you all of the facts nor is he required to do so.

The broker can add the number of winners (500 + 250+125 and so on) and come out with a final number of 999. The broker can then claim that, out of 1000 *players* there were 999 winners making his system as close to a "sure thing" as you can get. Right?

But, the actual numbers also tell you that 999 *players* lost $, and that one *player* out of a thousand was lucky enough to be the recipient of 10 lucky guesses. He also didn't tell you the fees and commissions and taxes involved in processing those bets. So, the true winner was the broker, especially with the book deal!

By focusing on the Eagle's Eye view, he can make a negative situation (999 out of 1000 lose) into a great situation (999 winners out of 1000 *players*, or picking 10 straight winners). And to that one lone *player*, the broker is a genius who helped make him wealthy.

According to the rules governing the markets, if this strategy is applied knowingly and with intent to defraud, it is illegal. However, the burden of proof is on the *player* who never has all the necessary information. What happens in the "Coin Flip Method" is the same thing that happens millions of times a day in the markets as brokers claim they can predict an unpredictable in your favor. Brokers are not trained to understand the markets and pick the best stocks, because there is no system. They are salesmen helping insecure investors try to turn a little $ into a lot of $ without effort. They're predicting a non-predictable, and if you still don't believe me, just remember these words:

"Past performance does not predict future results"

How brokers use the Eagle's Eye view to manipulate statistics
Let me give you an example of how brokers mislead you to give you a false sense of security in playing the markets.

Crazyman's View

Example 1
Player A purchased a share of stock from a company for $100

	(out of pocket $)		(in pocket $)
Player A	$ 100	sells to Player B for	$ 110
Player B	$ 110	sells to Player C for	$ 120
Player C	$ 120	sells to Player D for	$ 130
Player D	$ 130		
Total out of pocket	$ 460		
Total in-pocket			$ 360
Total out of pocket			**-$ 100**

In this example, Player A, B and C all made $ (after fees and commissions), and Player D is -$130. *Players* as a whole are -$100 + expenses.

Example 2
Player A purchased a share of stock from a company for $100

	(out of pocket $)		(in pocket $)
Player A	$ 100	sells to Player B for	$ 90
Player B	$ 90	sells to Player C for	$ 80
Player C	$ 80	sells to Player D for	$ 70
Player D	$ 70		
Total out of pocket	$ 340		
Total in-pocket			$ 240
Total out of pocket			**-$ 100**

In this example, all *players* have lost $. Player D is -$70. *Players* as a whole are -$100 + expenses.

Example 3
Player A purchased a share of stock from a company for $100

	(out of pocket $)		(in pocket $)
Player A	$ 100	sells to Player B for	$ 100
Player B	$ 100	sells to Player C for	$ 100
Player C	$ 100	sells to Player D for	$ 100
Player D	$ 100		
Total out of pocket	$ 400		
Total in-pocket			$ 300
Total out of pocket			**-$ 100**

In this example, all four *players* lost $ once you take out fees and commissions. The broker would avoid showing you this, but if he did, he would claim this is a zero-sum gain, but in fact, it is a minus-sum game. And the company got the $, and Player D is -$100. *Players* as a whole are -$100 + expenses.

Example 4
Player A purchased a share of stock from a company for $100

	(out of pocket $)		(in pocket $)
Player A	$ 100	sells to Player B for	$ 90
Player B	$ 90	sells to Player C for	$ 100
Player C	$ 100	sells to Player D for	$ 90
Player D	$ 90		
Total out of pocket	$ 380		
Total in-pocket			$ 280
Total out of pocket			**-$ 100**

In this example, Player B makes $10, but Player A, C and D are minus $110 (plus added fees and commissions). When the broker explains this, he would show that Player B made $10, and Player D has a $90 value. *Players* as a whole are -$100 + expenses.

To clarify, the $ the publicly traded company receives from the sale of a share is never reclaimed. Fees and commissions are factored into every transaction (motion). In every example above, there is no denying that it is a minus-sum game.

Notice the simple math of the system. You can add layer upon layer of complexity and terminology, but it always comes back to simple math. That's the minus-sum game, and it's impossible for *players* as a whole to beat the system.

The broker will confidently point to the three *players* in Example 1 and point out how they made $. The fourth *player* has possession of a stock which has seen steady growth. The reality is that Player D has spent $130 and has a piece of paper that has published value. He has in his hand the greatest illusion of actual wealth. By focusing on the Eagle's Eye view of individual performance, an illusion is created that *Players* A, B & C made $30, and Player D has $130 value. It looks like a positive outcome, but the *players* are out $100, plus fees and commissions, and Player D is holding an empty bag.

Player D represents the millions of *players* in this country that hold approximately $15 Trillion of published-value stocks today. They have paper with published value and no actual $ in pocket. What will happen to all of the Player D's of the world? They pawn off their stock to Player E, and the game goes on with created motion. But there'll always be someone who will end up holding paper with published value and no real $.

Players spend time studying financial reports that may or may not be accurate. They are almost certainly outdated. All of the news reports and stock market analysis on certain companies can be

Crazyman $ays:
"If you are willing to bear the responsibility of your advice, you are worth listening to."

studied, but when their analysis is wrong (as it is more often than not), they can claim that past performance does not predict future results.

So, when your broker is working in your best interest and tells you to invest in an S&P 500® company he judges "safe," you have no more chance of your money being secure than any other stock. As we saw earlier, S&P 500® is just a statistical point of reference that the industry uses and offers no true value.

If you bring up the losses you, or another *player*, incurs, brokers will blame the *player's* inept actions, citing Caveat Emptor (let the buyer beware). Or the player was being greedy and stupid. Why blame the broker who only offered his advice? The *player* wasn't fully educated on the ups and downs of the markets so of course the *player* will lose $ when he acts on his own or when the market forces are in flux. The broker is merely a salesman who only provides advice how to best spend your $. You should be responsible enough to do your own research, because you decide to buy what they're selling. This is hogwash.

Brokers always tell you there's a risk, but also leave out key information. They use psychological tricks to play upon your ego or your search for security. They use well-tested sales techniques and manipulation to get you to put your $ in motion. And while others may have lost $, it was surely due to the *player* being poorly educated and relying on bad information. But hey, if you play the game right, you will win. Then they use a combination of disclaimers, disclaimers,

and more disclaimers to remove liability
if they get caught sharing bad
information.

And this information results in you
playing that minus-sum game.

The MASTERS have succeeded in
creating such a complex system, that not
only do a select few understand how it
functions, but you need a license to
actually conduct business with the
exchanges. The key is when a broker's
advice becomes bad advice, they place
the blame on the *player* for acting on
their advice. They also avoid liability
under the rules set up by the Security
and Exchange Commission (SEC) and the
National Futures Association (NFA).

Despite all that you hear about how
brokers have to be licensed and face a
mountain of laws and regulations in
order to protect the *player*, the rules are
actually designed to protect the
organizations from the *players*. So an
amateur is held responsible even when
their losses can be attributed to advice
they received from a professional.

Don't count on the regulatory
commissions to protect you as a *player*.
The commissions need the exchanges to
be in business to have a job to do.

The true purpose of the regulatory
commissions are to:
►   ensure the exchanges are successful;
►   ensure the winners get their $;
►   ensure the losers can't hold the
    brokers or exchanges liable;
►   ensure the brokers and exchanges
    are not required to keep any records
    negative to their success.

Let's say laws were enacted that allowed brokers to be charged with malpractice. Your broker or $ manager would tell you in detail about every risk involved in handing them your $ from the volatility of the markets to how it's impossible for anyone to beat the system long term. Every disclaimer would be spelled out for you in person, and you would be told the percentage of success or failure. If brokers had these standards, *players* would have a far better understanding of what was happening with their $. It would also greatly reduce the number of *players* which would cripple the Fat Cats, which is why it will never happen.

Record of players' $

Change will only be brought about when *players* demand full disclosure and accountability. Brokers and exchanges promote the fact that they are tightly regulated, but they are not required to keep or disclose simple information that would inform *players* that they are entering a minus-sum game.

True story:
I asked my accountant to get a record of *players'* $ from a broker for a major financial institution. The broker responded to his request by asking my accountant who I was, why I wanted this information, that I didn't need that information, and that he wouldn't give it to me anyway. The broker then told my accountant he should fire me as a client for asking such questions. Why would he be so unwilling to provide the information to the point of suggesting my accountant fire me?

It isn't complicated. I wanted accountability, pure and simple. What I got was a classic example of how the brokers and exchanges are not required to provide any information that would be detrimental to their success. A record of *players'* $ would show *players* where their $ goes and where it comes from. It would demand full disclosure and accountability from those people that handle *players'* finances.

If record of *players*' $ existed, they would detail:
▶ how the *players*' $ was distributed;
▶ how much $ the company received;
▶ how much in fees and commissions were charged off the top by the brokers and exchanges;
▶ how much the IRS collects;
▶ how many *players* made $; and
▶ how much and how many *players* lost $ and how much.

A record of *players*' $ would expose the illusion that *players*, as a whole, are benefiting from the stock market. The fact is that the majority of *players* are losing $. But the MASTERS have conditioned us to trust the process, and we don't ask for information we wouldn't get anyway. What would a level playing field look like?

It's impossible in a minus-sum game to have more winners than losers as a whole. So, no matter how good a system is, they have to produce more losers to support the winners as a whole. If any financial planner was required to provided you with a performance report, it would have to show that more *players* lost $ than made $.
Remember that when you are dealing with a broker, he is part of the plan of the MASTERS whether he is consciously aware of it or not. Whether your broker has your best interests in mind, the system itself is an elaborate con. *Players* are participating in a minus-sum game. And brokers do not have to provide an accounting of who wins $ and who loses $.

Yearly Personal Report

Client Name:_____

Acct #:_____

Out of pocket expenses:	$_____
In pocket expenses:	$_____

A. Out of Pocket expenses	B. In pocket expenses
Purchases _____	Sales _____
Fees _____	Settlements _____
Commissions _____	Dividends _____
Total A_____ B_____	Total B_____ A_____
Total money out of pocket N_____ (Negative cash flow)	Total money in pocket P_____ (Positive cash flow)
If A is bigger than B Subtract B from A	If B is bigger than A Subtract A from B

This information is an accurate accounting of the
client's yearly transactions.

Broker Name: _____

Signature:_____

(note: This does not factor in taxes)
Each year, the exchanges would be required to
provide this information to each client.

Chapter Ten:
— The face of the con —

This chapter is based on the article "Evolution of an Investor" by Michael Lewis in the December, 2007 issue of *Portfolio Magazine*.

I wasn't interested in including a lot of references in the book because I felt that they either didn't get it or they didn't tell me anything new. One day while we were working on the book, I stopped in the bank to sign some papers and picked up the December 2007, issue of *Portfolio* magazine. I read the profile on Blaine Lourd written by Michael Lewis and realized that this man supports my argument.

"The stock market has no use for human wisdom and judgment."

From the article "Evolution of an Investor" by Michael Lewis in the December, 2007 issue of *Portfolio Magazine*.

I encourage you to go to the website (portfolio.com) and read the story. It tells you everything you need to know about the market through the eyes of a gentleman named Blaine Lourd. Through his eyes you can see how Wall Street really is. He says, "Wall Street, with its army of brokers, analysts, and advisers funneling trillions of dollars into mutual funds, hedge funds, and private equity funds, is an elaborate fraud." While he tells you it's a scam and con, he is also weaving a web to bring you into his new fund.

Lourd shows an inclination to be a con man when he admits that he wanted to be a success. How that happened, he didn't much care. He left Louisiana when his father's oil business, his anticipated inheritance, collapsed. He landed his first job at EF Hutton and prepared himself by learning how to peddle stocks to people he'd never met. The key was to bring up Warren Buffett's name early and often. Lourd himself points out that he never understood why his customers never fired him. Before long, he began taking the investors for granted. According to Lourd: "You had to get the second deal done before the first one went bad." And the first one always went bad. His boss told Lourd that his job was to turn his clients' net worth into his own. It was amazing to him how gullible the *players* were.

His fortunes change when the business manager of the rock band, the Rolling Stones, gave him $13 million to invest. He decided to forgo his bosses' advice and put it into T-bills. Even though this was a secure investment for the band, this brought in little revenue for the firm. His bosses told him his decision didn't make any money for them, and they pressured him to make transactions rather than give what he considered safe investment advice asked for by his clients, the Rolling Stones. I would think that Lourd made the best decision for his clients, but as you can see, the only goal was to keep the $ in motion to generate fees and commissions.

Lourd makes several admissions throughout the article. He talked about how much money managers make, but

how, as a group, they cannot outperform
the market. He admitted that he, like
many of his successful counterparts,
abused drugs and alcohol due in no
small part to the guilt they have over
taking advantage of their clients. "You
can't continually hurt people and feel
good about yourself," he mused. Lourd
admitted that becoming a success in
this industry was reason enough to
hate himself.

In an amazing admission of societies'
permissiveness of the industry, no CEO
at any bank that Lourd worked for, no
money manager or director, no chairman
of the board and no associates ever
asked him how his clients were doing.
They just congratulated him periodically
on his high gross commissions.
Through all of his work with major Wall
Street firms, the nicest thing Lourd
could say about himself is that he hadn't
broken the law. He recalls the times
he spent making people happy about
his advice when they should have been
furious. Lourd says: "I always thought
there would be a place where the
clients and the brokers wouldn't be
compromised. But it was the same
everywhere." He was in the top 10 of
revenue producers for in every firm that
employed him, but his success was not
based on making successful investment
decisions. He said he worked harder than
everyone else to bring new *players* into
the game.

More and more, Lourd said, he saw Wall
Street as part of an elaborate fraud. He
was one of those who funneled trillions
of dollars into hedge funds, mutual
funds and private equity funds, all the

time growing less and less confident in his ability to pick winning stocks or money managers.

The illusion that professional investment managers can beat the market is proven false time and time again throughout the article. Blaine read Charles Ellis' book, "The Losers Game." Ellis said there is no such thing as a financial expert. Blaine figured out that the problem wasn't him or the firms where he worked. The problem was the entire system of Wall Street, in which people presented themselves as financial experts and were paid extravagant sums of money for their "knowledge."

Ellis argued there was no such thing as financial expertise. As Lourd read the book, he realized his whole life is a lie. "Everyone around me is facilitating this lie." Lourd was in the top 30 out of 6000 Edward Jones employees. Then he went to work for A.G. Edwards and began telling his clients he shouldn't pick stocks for them or dump their money into actively managed mutual funds. Instead, he chose to put it all in index funds. For this service, he took an annual fee of one percent of their assets. A. G. Edwards was not happy with his decision. Even the United States Government and the SEC wanted him to keep his accounts in constant motion. At that point, Lourd said, "I was done."

This is an important crossroads. In Hollywood, the story would turn out that the lead character would leave Wall Street and spend the rest of his career working to fix a corrupt system. But, this isn't Hollywood. The amazing thing is after all of the disillusionment of his association with the market, Lourd starts his own firm and contacts a firm to invest his funds.

The firm, Dimensional Fund Advisors (DFA), sold *players* on the idea of passive investing. Founded in 1981, the firm was founded on a simple idea: Nobody knows which stock is going to go up. Nobody knows what the market as a whole is going to do. However honest their motto is, the fact that they are still drawing *players* into the markets indicates that they just figured out a better marketing plan.

According to the article, DFA bought and held baskets of stocks chosen for the sort of risk they represented. And they—along with the idea they embodied—were growing at a sensational rate. By the summer of 2007, the firm had an astonishing $153 billion under management, $90 billion of which had come from individual investors through a network of professional advisers.

Those preparing to join the thousands authorized to sell DFA's funds to investors imply their agreement. They're all salesmen, but salesmen peddling an odd idea: Don't listen to salesmen. DFA's entire firm premise is all about "Wall Street floats on bullshit." DFA employees never believe they possess special wisdom and judgment. As a *player*, this should tell you something.

Early on, at DFA, they did not sell individual stocks, try to time the market, or suggest to an investor that it is possible to systematically beat the

market. They sold *players* on the premise
that *players* can't beat the system, and
DFA can't beat the system, but they
wanted your $ anyway. And as one DFA
person said: "Who would be the most
efficient at taking investors who thinks he
can beat the system in the markets and
turn him into someone who quits trading
and hands their money over to DFA?"
The answer was easy. "Blaine Lourd."

I found it fascinating that Lourd himself
believes that in a perfect world, there
wouldn't be any stock brokers or mutual
fund managers. But he says the world is
not perfect. Lourd says people need to
believe that there's a guy, and that the
guy knows what to do with someone's
portfolio better than them. To him, that
guy might as well be Blaine Lourd.

What about investors that systematically
beat the market? The article emphasizes it
simply doesn't exist. If, by some miracle,
a *player* comes along that can beat the
market, it is the individual *player*, not
players as a whole, who will benefit.
Remember that good information given
to too many people becomes bad
information.

You are sold on the premise of the
importance of the markets, though at no
time in the article does Lourd talk about
the important economic function he was
contributing to, other than his own. That's
what the media's role is all about. They
tell a story every day about today's stock
returns. As the article states, "It's
businessman's pornography." If anyone
from Wall Street calls you up with
financial advice, you should be very
afraid. But it isn't fear that promotes
players to embrace DFA, its greed.

At the end of the profile, Lourd pulls out a chart on one of DFA's funds, (just one, because it wouldn't be beneficial for him to reveal true financial statistics) and shows how it outperformed Buffett's Hathaway funds.

There's a very nice picture of Lourd in the profile projecting a smiling, trustworthy face. He is very smart and handsome. Obviously he projects a winning personality. Lourd talks about how bad it is, but he keeps getting better and better at what he's doing. It proves that he doesn't really care. He is neither unique nor different. He's one of thousands. The photo of him reading the sports page, while a monkey reads the stock quotes, is as accurate a description of the market as the article itself. And yet, he's still in the game.

The article is yet another example of how the greatest con men will tell you what they do is a con, but still convince you that what they're working on now is legit.

Chapter Eleven:
— Publicly traded companies are private companies' worst enemy —

Why am I talking about public and private companies in a book about the markets? I believe a majority of *players* who purchase shares of a publicly traded company has no idea what an overall negative impact their action has on their own community. Publicly traded companies are harmful to the economy on both a local and national scale.

Think about it for a moment. How do publicly traded companies run private companies out of business? Most people believe behemoth-sized companies buy goods in higher volume at lower prices, at the same time offering significantly reduced prices to consumers. They also claim that vigorous competition is part of a capitalistic society. The problem is that neither one of these are accurate.

The main reason publicly traded companies run private companies out of business is through the use of free capital provided by shareholders.

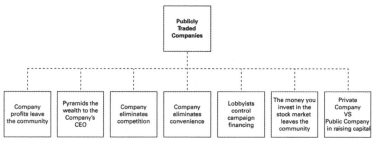

Publicly traded companies claim to be at a disadvantage as they have more regulations to satisfy. They have to spend more on accounting, bureaucratic paperwork, and filing reports such as the 10- K reports with the Security and Exchanges Commission. It is also argued that publicly traded companies are under more pressure to "make the numbers" because they have shareholders waiting for a return on their investment. Private corporations don't have to disclose such information and are not bound by the same regulations as publicly traded companies.

The seven ways publicly traded companies are bad for your community:

1. Publicly traded companies have a significant advantage in raising capital.
2. Company profits leave your community.
3. Pyramids the wealth to the company CEOs.
4. Company eliminates local competition.
5. Company eliminates convenience.
6. Company lobbyists control campaign financing.
7. Money you invest to buy stock in the company leaves the community.

These so-called advantages of a private company are minor compared to the major obstacles facing them in going up against a publicly traded company.

Here's a simple example: A private owner goes to the bank and gets a business loan for $10,000 for 10 years at six percent interest. At the end of the loan period, the owner would have repaid the principal of $10,000, plus $3,000 interest for $13,000 total.

A publicly traded company that sold $10,000 worth of shares doesn't have to pay the capital back, and only has an option to pay dividends which average out to about one percent a year. At the end of 10 years, the company would have paid out $1000 ($100/year for 10 years) in dividends. For our example, our hypothetical company was generous enough to pay dividends. Some companies choose not to pay any dividends at all.

The private company is out the principal, plus interest, totaling $13,000. The publicly traded company only loses the dividend, and leaves them with $9,000 of free capital. The publicly company has $9,000 of free capital, plus the private company has had to repay $13,000. The publicly traded company has a $22,000 advantage with the added benefit of free capital. Now, take that $10,000 and make it $10,000,000 and this shows the enormous advantage publicly traded companies have over private companies.

What other negative qualities do publicly traded companies present to the community? Due to their access to a large amount of free capital, a national retail chain (NRC) comes to a town with an instantly recognizable name. They build a gigantic store overnight and hold a carnival-like grand opening with severely slashed sale prices.

Good will, along with a customer base the private company has built over the years is immediately undermined. This is

Private Company VS Public Company

Bank lends $1,000 to a Private Company at 5% interest rate for 10 years expecting one payment per year. Private Company would have to pay $129 per year for the $1,000.
Amortization Calculator = $1,000 X 5% X 1 payment per year X 10 years

A Public Company would sell shares to generate $1,000 that would create nothing more than an expectation of hope for shareholders who might realize a 1% dividend.
1% of $1,000 = $10

	Year	How $1,000 is depreciated	Payment Due at End of Year	How much $ to work with
Private Company	1st	$1,000	$129	$871
	2nd	$871	$129	$742
	3rd	$742	$129	$613
	4th	$613	$129	$484
	5th	$484	$129	$355
	6th	$355	$129	$226
	7th	$226	$129	$97
	8th	$97	$129	($32)
	9th	($32)	$129	($161)
	10th	($161)	$129	($290)

	Year	How $1,000 is depreciated	Cost of Dividends paid to Shareholders	How much $ to work with
Public Company	1st	$1,000	$10	$990
	2nd	$990	$10	$980
	3rd	$980	$10	$970
	4th	$970	$10	$960
	5th	$960	$10	$950
	6th	$950	$10	$940
	7th	$940	$10	$930
	8th	$930	$10	$920
	9th	$920	$10	$910
	10th	$910	$10	$900

not done with profit or efficiency. These mega-stores are built on free capital. This process has forced many privately owned companies to close their doors.

I built a company from scratch, and I will tell you that competition is a vital function of Capitalism. I also believe competition is the consumers' greatest asset, until the goal of publicly traded companies becomes elimination of competition. When a national retail chain comes into town and builds a mega store, they are an immediate threat to locally owned competition, (drug stores, hardware stores, grocery stores, shoe stores, dress shops, etc).

As these smaller concerns fall, the consumer has fewer and fewer shopping choices. The variety of products available is confined to those offered by the mega store. The mega store becomes a magnet for shoppers in small surrounding towns, and, locally owned stores soon fail there. Within a very short time small town consumers lose their freedom of choice. They are forced to travel to NRC's centralized location to buy essential products available in the store.

In many cases, it's the business practices of the NRC that drive manufacturers out of business. They're so big that they can dictate terms of payment, short pays, short order, and delayed paying suppliers on invoices, so that it forces suppliers into a "no-win" situation. Here's an example: a supplier bills the NRC $10,000 for their goods. The NRC takes up to 90 days to pay the invoice, then when the payment arrives, the invoice is modified to include added "charges" the NRC incurred, and the check is for $7,500. The supplier has a choice to fight to get the other $2,500, at the risk of legal fees and possibly losing the NRC as a client, or simply to accept the losses and continue the relationship at a reduced profit margin. This is known as a "short pay."

Publicly traded companies have significant advantages that create an un-level playing field.

In some cases, the NRC dictates to the consumer and supplier both. If the NRC decides not to carry the product, the customer has no place to buy it, and the supplier has no one to sell it to so the NRC is actually limiting choice to their consumers by controlling the market. In a free market, the consumer should always be in control. In this case, it's taken out of the hands of the consumer and put in the hands of the NRC.

There is no motivation for the NRC to purchase products locally or even nationally. It has forced some large manufacturers to relocate out of the United States to lower production costs below what can realistically occur in the United States at the costs of our local manufacturers.

On the local level, the NRC takes all of their administrative, management, and marketing functions and profit and moves it to their home office. The $ that local people spend on shares of the NRC goes to the home office and is not reinvested in the community. The NRC, in many instances, pays their employees a wage that is lower than average, reducing the standard of living in the town.

In a privately owned company, the management, marketing, and administrative expenses, as well as the profit, would remain in the community with local people put to work. Suppliers have more opportunities to sell their goods. Consumers decide what and where to purchase. Stronger local economies are created with more options for consumers and for suppliers.

Why are private companies more
efficient than publicly traded companies?
Private companies have to earn a profit.
Borrowed $ has to be repaid with those
profits. Owners who don't build a wide
customer base, who don't offer customer
services, and desirable products don't
earn a profit. There will be no golden
parachute or obscene performance
bonus for these business owners.

You see the enormous advantage that
publicly traded companies have over the
private sector. With free capital, they can
work on a much smaller profit margin –
or no margin at all. So they can discount
their products and gain the advantage
over their private sector competitors.

They accomplish this feat at the expense
of the shareholders.

More importantly, a private company is
most likely locally owned, and it
conducts a majority of its business within
the community. Customer good will is
paramount. The publicly traded company
is far less likely to invest in the
community. The community has a false
sense of security by the appearance of
the publicly traded company with its
glitzy store, promise of employment, and
foremost, cheap prices. As I said before,
the search for security is the greatest
threat to our freedoms.

The publicly traded company has to
answer to the scrutiny of "Wall Street,"
which spends countless hours and $
analyzing, speculating, and anticipating
what the quarterly reports will show
next. Despite what we know about the
con, companies pay special interest and

react to what they think will result in a
more favorable report.

I'm going to show you why today's
business practices are not only bad for
the private sector, but for the economy
as a whole. As we discussed, publicly
traded companies have more expenses
within their corporate structure. They also
have to contend with the increased rules
and regulations. They also don't have to
show a consistent profit to continue with
business as usual.

Publicly traded companies don't repay
the collected principal provided by
shareholders. To level the playing field
with private companies, publicly owned
companies would have to pay
approximately 12 percent dividends.
Shareholders would be ecstatic, and
private companies would have a better
chance to compete.

This 12 percent sounds like a lot of $,
but since the *players* provided the
principal with no guarantee of a return,
this does not seem like an unreasonable
option. Now, how many publicly traded
companies do you know that pay out
a consistent 12 percent dividend?
Since this would put publicly traded
companies on the same level as private
sector companies where there would be
true competition, it won't happen any
time soon.

With all of the misinformation about
benefits to the community that NRC
brings, the consumer ultimately pays the
price. The community loses in the end.
When inefficient companies run more
efficient companies out of business,

it has an overall negative effect on the economy.

Reality—CEOs have an ace up their sleeve

The CEO of a publicly traded company is given opportunities to make a fortune by taking advantage of stock options being issued in their own company. The argument is that by getting stock options as part of their overall compensation package, the CEO is motivated to make the company more successful to bring up the stock price. But, if a CEO simply wants to make as much $ as possible from the stock options, it doesn't always have to occur from the success of the company.

Here's a hypothetical scenario of how a CEO is able to manipulate the system to their advantage. A CEO's company (Company X) has shares listed on the NYSE with a published value of $20/share, and the CEO, along with a group of insiders, want Company X's stocks to drop to a published value of $10/share.

The CEO puts a secret plan in action to intentionally make the company look bad through poor performance and excess spending. The CEO, through a series of executive decisions, cuts the sales force, increases the budget for unnecessary personnel and equipment. Increased expenses and decreased sales raise costs and lower profits. It's possible even to manipulate statistics to artificially deflate the value of the company.

When Company X suddenly shows a dramatic loss in profits, the stock drops

Crazyman $ays:
"A record of players' $
would expose the illusion
that players, as a whole,
are benefiting from
the stock market."

to a published value of $10/share as a result of the perception of poor performance.

The CEO is forced out through retirement or termination. Either way he leaves with a lavish severance package that includes stock options to purchase a million shares of Company X stock at its current published value of $10/share.

The outgoing CEO has confidence in the new CEO who has a reputation for turning companies around. Let's say the shares increase to a published value of $15/share, he can still buy them at $10/share and automatically has a $5/share profit advantage over other *players*. If he buys it under value, it devalues the other shareholders that purchased it at a published value of $15/share.

The former CEO decides to exercise his options to buy his million shares of stocks at $10/share. Company X now has $10 million of additional capital.

The new CEO of Company X immediately builds market confidence by cutting the payroll and reducing expenses as well as increasing the sales force and instituting new sales programs. Company X once again shows growth and profit through this well-executed plan. The stock increases in published value up to $25/share.

In this scenario, the former CEO pockets $ at any point he decides to find other *players* to purchase his Company X shares at a published price above $10/share. When he decides to sell, he makes a million dollars profit for every dollar the share goes up above $10/share.

This may be an overly simplistic example, but I can assure you the level of deception that goes on is far more complex and devious. The results are the same.

It's scandalous that publicly traded companies are allowed to pay stock options and excessive salaries to CEOs whether they deserved them or not. Employees, without insider information, shouldn't accept stock options as part of their benefit package. CEOs that have insider information should be denied stock options in their own companies as it creates an obvious conflict-of-interest. The Security and Exchange Commission has required increased disclosure of CEO compensation packages, but this has had only a slight effect.

The key here is that *players* and employees lose because the excess salaries paid to CEO's come directly from the shareholders with no accountability. The board of directors doesn't care – it's not their money. The SEC allows boards of directors free reign to set salaries as they see fit. The real scandal, as we discussed earlier, is that CEOs are rewarded as much for the poor performance of their company as for a strong performance.

The myth of the "compassionate CEO"
Bill Gates of Microsoft made news in late 2007 by encouraging his colleagues in the business world to become more of a compassionate CEO that directs more of

their profits to help the developing third-world countries. Mr. Gates himself in the past has committed himself to give away most of his fortune to those in need oversees. While at first glance, this appears commendable, there's a problem with this plan. Microsoft didn't pay dividends for years, and the dividend payout, according to the information on the Microsoft investor relations website (as of March 1, 2008) is 1.55%. At this rate, it would take over 66 years to pay shareholders for their principal.

Gates needs to pay dividends to his shareholders who helped make him a billionaire before he starts giving it away. He's not giving away his $ but giving away his shareholders' $.

The bottom line is that by playing the stock market and buying shares in a publicly traded company, you are handing the company your $ you won't get back for them to use as free capital to spend as they wish. But, more importantly, you are contributing to an increasing problem of these publicly traded companies pushing out the private companies and reducing choices for the consumer.

Chapter Twelve:
—Yearly personal reports —

Throughout this book, I have repeatedly asked why the brokers and exchanges are not required to produce any reports of *players'* $. I think it's time that we demand from our elected officials that all participants have to provide full accountability of how much $ *players* have spent out-of-pocket on investments, fees, commissions, and estimated taxes.

Here's my simple solution: The following three reports would show a detailed accounting of each individual *players'* $, brokers' performance as a whole, and the exchange with all participants as a whole. The broker and exchange reports would be required to be published yearly and available to anyone upon request and the yearly personal report would be confidential.

Broker performance report on total clients	
Broker Name:_____	
Firm:_____	
Year:_____Signature:_____	
Number of clients with positive Cash Flow: _____	Number of clients with negative Cash Flow: _____
Total amount in pocket: $_____	Total amount in pocket: $_____
This report is made public every year.	

Exchanges performance report on total clients

Name:_____ _____

Year:_____

Number of clients with positive Cash Flow: _____	Number of clients with negative Cash Flow: _____
Total amount in pocket: $_____	Total amount in pocket: $_____

This report is made public every year.

Confidential Yearly Personal Report

Client Name:_____

Acct #:_____

Out of pocket expenses: $_____

In pocket expenses: $_____

A. Out of Pocket expenses	B. In pocket expenses
Purchases _____	Sales _____
Fees _____	Settlements _____
Commissions _____	Dividends _____
Total A_____ B_____	Total B_____ A_____
Total money out of pocket N_____ (Negative cash flow)	Total money in pocket P_____ (Positive cash flow)
If A is bigger than B Subtract B from A	If B is bigger than A Subtract A from B

This information is an accurate accounting of the client's yearly transactions.

Broker Name: _____

Signature:_____

I did not factor in the negative cash flow of the taxes collected or deducted by the IRS. These charts would go a long way towards providing *players* with an honest accountability of their $.

If these reports were required and made public today, how many of you would still be confident in the markets, and would this book would still be necessary?

Chapter Thirteen:
— You may not beat the system, but you can quit losing $ —

Unlike a majority of books and articles that dare question the markets, I have no "magic solution." There is no way to beat the system. The purpose of the book was to tell you the dangers of the markets, and expose the pitfalls of Wall Street and the commodities exchanges, and show that your investments and retirement is in jeopardy.

My dad told me years ago that a man who has $ in his pocket will eat that night. One who doesn't might go hungry. I may be a common man, and I went to the school of hard knocks and graduated at the head of the class with a DA's (dumb ass) degree and majored in CM (counting $). But it was this real-life education that led me to not believe what I had been told or taught. I followed my $ and did my math. Facts are facts.

This is what we've learned about buying and selling shares in publicly traded companies and contracts in the commodities contracts:

▶ It is a minus-sum game;
▶ Not only is it a minus-sum game, but 95 percent of *players* as a whole lose $;
▶ Prices are not determined on any mathematical or scientific formula;

Crazyman $ays:
"If the losers quit losing…
the lights would go out!"

▶ Prices are created on the consensus of the buyers and sellers trying to predict an unpredictable;
▶ The prices change constantly;
▶ *Players* can buy and sell by the second;
▶ This buying and selling creates volatility;
▶ The volatility creates motion;
▶ The motion takes $ out of pockets of *players* (-$) and puts $ into the pockets of Fat Cats;
▶ The volatility makes it possible for *players* to believe they can turn a little $ into a lot of $ quickly.

This system was developed and perfected over the years by the Masters of Illusion and Deception. They designed this con game to separate generations of Americans from their $ without having any accountability or prosecution.

To put this system into place, the MASTERS had to change the reality that the markets are gambling and to create the perception that the markets are a vital economic function for the masses. To do this, they had to concoct an image that *players*, by participating, can:
▶ make $;
▶ achieve financial security;
▶ contribute to a vital and important economic function;
▶ take responsibility for their own losses.

In the process, the MASTERS knew they had to develop a system so complex that the news media, the academic community, the federal officials, and the public wouldn't understand it while they accepted it without question. The system itself was designed to such an extent that the burden of responsibility is placed on the *players* to be accountable for their losses. As it was so complex and difficult to understand, the federally elected officials needed to set up self-regulated commissions to oversee and manage the markets. They effectively put the fox in charge of the hen house.

We now know the role of the regulatory commissions of the commodities market and stock markets are:
▶ to make sure the winners get their $;
▶ to make rules that ensure the success of the organization;
▶ to make sure losers have no legal recourse;
▶ to not keep any records that would endanger the success of the organization.

The commissions set up rules preventing losers from seeking retribution or holding the exchanges liable for their losses. Through this process, the *player* is conditioned to accept all responsibility for losses. As long as the rules are followed, there's no recourse for justice through the exchanges, and the *player* ultimately must live with the results. By accepting responsibility for their losses, *players* fail to seek action from our federally elected officials to force the exchanges to provide full accountability for *players'* $.

Once they got control of the system through self-regulation, the MASTERS worked to prevent any rules that would provide full disclosure and accountability. They could avoid keeping any records or publishing any statistics that would

hold them accountable to *players*.
Nothing detrimental to the system is
disclosed. They are now in control of a
system designed to ensure successful
market exchanges.

Through deception, the MASTERS
succeeded in making you believe the
illusion that *players* are not gambling,
but they are performing a legitimate
economic function to secure their
financial futures. The news media,
academic world, and federally elected
officials all fell in line and promoted that
premise without question.

Next, the MASTERS created a series of
games which enticed *players* as a whole
into thinking they could turn a little $ into
a lot of $ without effort. In order to
maintain the illusion that *players* were
investing, they added terms of value to
their games. The games were disguised
as a business function when in fact it
was simply a contest where a *player* tries
to outguess other *players* in predicting a
non-predictable.

I have proven that the MASTERS created
a system that ensures that the brokers
and exchanges have a constant flow of $
coming in through motion. As Warren
Buffet's Fourth Law of Motion says: "As
motion increases, investors' returns
decreases." The more you play, the more
$ you lose.

This creates a minus-sum game for
players. While this should be obvious to
even the most experienced *players*, they
persist in believing the deception that the
markets are a zero-sum gain. When you
add in fees, commissions, taxes, and

other expenses, *players* as a whole wind up with less $ in pocket at the end of the day then before they started. As the market presently functions, all *players*, as a whole, will lose $ in time.

Mathematically, more losers, than winners, guarantee that markets will survive. We've been sold on the illusion of "published value," when in reality there is no $ to back it up. Unless you find another *player* to pay you to take over the contract, your paper is worthless. The term "perceived value" is what you believe you can get in return, but it has no basis for actual worth. Both of these terms are words of illusion with *players* placed in a very dangerous position.

In addition, "outperformed" is a misleading term used to make a bad situation look good and a good situation look better. It can mean anything the broker wants it to, but it has no true reference point. Outperformed doesn't provide anything unless full disclosure is provided. It is just a manipulation of statistics formulated to increase *player* confidence.

The MASTERS created a system that benefited themselves and the Fat Cats. However, side effects produced negatives to consumers. First, in the commodities market, prices have to range between reasonable profit and out of the market. Therefore, the consumer can only get reasonable profit and above which is negative to the consumer.

Another side effect allows use of free capital by publicly traded companies after they collected it from shareholders.

Crazyman $ays:
"The purpose of
this book is...
Get the losers to quit
losing!"

Private companies find it impossible to compete using traditional business loans. Both stock markets and commodity markets are the *players'* worst enemies. Both markets as a whole are negative to the economy.

The commodity markets promote the fact that they are able to manage price risk through reflecting and discovering prices, not by setting them. This is a very important distinction since it removes any responsibility of high prices from the producers and places it on the market. But they claim that high prices are due to factors outside the control of the markets. This is actually contradictory in nature. Do their claims provide an important economic function by keeping prices lower for the consumer? This is the key illusion and deception the MASTERS use.

What can we do?
▶ Stop the losers in the markets from losing
▶ Take the gambling out of the markets

1. **We need to stop the losers from losing**
   For once the losers are in control. This is area in which we don't need any new laws or help from our federal elected officials. There's no way to beat the system when *players* are participating in a minus-sum game. The only sure way for *players* to quit losing is to quit participating in the two largest con games in U.S. history...the stock market and commodity markets. How can that be bad for the economy?

2. We need to take the gambling out of the markets

Gambling is ultimately a losing game. Despite the lure of easy money, the markets depend on the losers to survive.

Therefore, to remove the gambling from the markets, this is what we need our federal elected officials to do:

▶ limit the ability to trade from hundreds of times a year to 12 times per year.;

▶ Do away with margins.

The exchanges need to enact rules that state that once you purchase a share or contract, you can sell them at anytime. However, you must hold it for at least 30 days to reap a profit.

The commodity exchanges need to eliminate margins. This would eliminate the gambling aspect of earning approximately 20 times the true value.

These two reforms would remove the gambling aspect from the markets by eliminating the lure of turning a little $ into a lot of $ quickly.

I hope you have questioned the necessity of the markets and are prepared to take steps to take your $ out of the hands of the Fat Cats. I called them Fat Cats, because it's a term we're all familiar with, but in truth, they are nothing more than parasites. The one thing I'm certain of is they have targeted you as their prey.

Since this system employs hundreds of thousands of people across several industries, there will be every effort to do whatever it takes in the name of self-preservation. I expect to be attacked, questioned, threatened, and dismissed as being a "conspiracy nut" by those who will attempt to discredit me. I might be vilified as "anti-American." I will certainly be accused of being ignorant of the system by not presenting a complex and confusing thesis full of dull research in order to impress a few and confuse the many. I will be censured for presenting a doomsday scenario leading to the suggestion that everyone quit buying stock and commodities. It will be said my philosophies will lead to an economic collapse and a return to the stone-age. To hold on to the status quo every attempt will be made to scare you with talk about the dangers of a shrinking market.

I'm 67 years old, and I've spend the last four years trying to understand the stock market and commodity markets. It comes down to this:

The MASTERS math of motion (mMm): The MASTERS put your $ in motion, and the simple fact is that the Fat Cats win, and *players* lose.

Now you know what they didn't want you to know. To ignore or dismiss this is just plain "crazy." If the losers will quit losing, the lights will go out.

And where should you put your money? It's up to you, but I would recommend that you don't ever put your money where it's not guaranteed. If you do, you give the Fat Cats the right to steal it without recourse. It comes down to this, do you trust the MASTERS?

Addendum One:
— Questions your broker won't answer,
with answers that your broker won't want to admit —

Go ask your broker for a report on *players' $*. When you get the runaround, ask these questions:

What is your job as a broker?

What is the average return on investments on public related company stocks?

Are there guarantees that I won't lose my $?

Are there any guarantees that I can sell my shares or contacts?

What is the average dividend paid on outstanding stock?

Where does the $ come from when I sell my shares or contacts?

What is the average life of a publicly traded company on the stock market?

If I lose $, whose fault is it?

Does your job as a broker depend on *players* losing $?

What do companies do with the $ they get from investors? Do they pay it back?

Why does it say on the stock certificates, they "have no par value?"

When I lose my $ by selling my share or contracts, do brokers and $ managers get penalized or reprimanded by the Security and Exchange Commission (SEC) or the National Futures Association (NFA)?

How are prices on shares or contacts determined?

How is margin $ in the commodities market divided up?

What percentage of *players* makes $?

Can I go to the bank and borrow $ to buy shares or contacts?

Is there any accounting system on how stock prices or commodities contracts are established?

Do you keep records on *players* $?

Are CEO stock options a positive or negative to the average *player*?

The last time I checked, a seat on the NYSE sold for $4 million. Does a NYSE seat holder hold any advantages over the average *player*? What about seats on the mercantile exchanges?

Is trading shares or contracts a zero sum gain? With expenses, does it become a minus sum gain?

The stock market collects $ for companies that they don't pay back. Brokers and $ managers make $. The IRS makes $ along with 5% of *player*s. Where does all of that $ come from?

If losers quit losing, what would happen to the markets?

Why aren't brokers and $ managers required to keep records of *player*s' $ and publish the statistics?

The published "value" of all outstanding stock is approximately $15 trillion. How much of that $ is put back into our economy through *players*?

What percentage of commodities contracts is actually delivered?

Is a *player's* cash flow worse when the market is open or closed?

Do you have any idea on how much $ *players* have made or lost in the commodity market and the stock market in the prior year?

How much new stock shares were issued in the past calendar year?

If, in a 401(k) you began playing at age 18, and you retire at age 65, which is 47 years, what is the percentage of publicly traded companies would last for those 47 years?

Can you tell me how much $ all your *players* made as a whole last year?

At the end of each day, do *players* as a whole have less $ in their pocket than they started with?

How much $ did *players* lose in selling publicly traded stocks or commodities contracts to other *players*?

What was the percentage of losers to winners in the markets? Can you tell me how much $ your clients lost last year?

These are the answers you should receive:

"9-out-of-10 *players* will lose some or all of their $."

"You are entering into a game of chance. You are trying to out-predict other *players.*"

"There is no possible way *players* as a whole can make $."

"When stock is issued, the company keeps the $ and doesn't pay it back."

"If all things were equal, all investors would lose $ in time."

"The markets are supported by losers. If the losers quit losing $, I would be out of a job."

"If you make $ selling your stock, the $ comes from another investor, not the company."

"To investors as a whole, there are only two positive cash flows, company buy backs (approximately one percent of the time) and dividends (paying approximately one-three percent)"

"No one knows how all of that margin $ is divided up."

"I don't keep performance records so I can't tell you if my clients made $ or lost $ investing."

"My job is to keep your $ moving, not to worry about your losses."

"I make my $ off fees and commissions, not the success of your investments."

"I make $, even if you don't."

"When you buy shares or contracts, there are no guarantees that you can sell them or what price you will receive."

"You are my source of income, but if you lose $ selling your shares or contracts, it is your own fault."

"*Players* buying and selling shares and contracts is a zero-sum gain. This means that at the end of the day, *players* as a whole have no more or no less $ than they started with."

"When you add commissions and transaction fees, it becomes a minus-sum gain. This means that at the end of the day, *players* lose $."

"Only positive cash flow to shareholders is considered dividends. Dividends are less then one percent."

"If companies buy back their shares, that is considered a positive cash flow to investors. Company buy backs are approximately one percent."

"CEO stock options are a negative to average investors."

"People with a seat on the exchanges have a built-in advantage over the average *player*. If they didn't why would they pay for the seat?"

"The average life of a publicly traded company is eight years."

"You as a *player* pay the wages for exchanges, brokers and $ managers."

"The IRS takes $ from the winners."

"The job of the SEC and NFA is to see that exchanges are successful. Losers are responsible for losses, not the exchanges, brokers or $ managers."

Addendum Two:
— Crazyman's Glossary —

Crazyman $ays: "Gambling is risking something of value in hopes of gaining something of more value on a non-predictable outcome, with the odds favoring the house."

Crazyman $ays: "Thinking about winning is how we get trapped into losing."

Crazyman $ays: "Our search for security is the greatest threat to our freedoms."

Crazyman $ays: "Gamblers don't count their losses, they only count their winnings."

Crazyman $ays: "If all things are equal, all *players* will lose $ over time."

Crazyman $ays: "Losing is the foreplay of winning."

Crazyman $ays: "Wall St. separates you from your $ by using three C's, Camouflage, Conditioning and Convincing."

Crazyman $ays: "I've never had a rich man call me to share his wealth. Plenty of people have called to help us both get rich off of my $."

Crazyman $ays: "The MASTERS don't share the good deals, they market the bad ones."

Crazyman $ays: "The goal of the MASTERS is to create a dependent *player*, not an informed *player*."

Crazyman $ays: "Remember: It's the information you don't get which is the most important."

Crazyman $ays: "Good information given to too many people becomes bad information."

Crazyman $ays: "Motion takes $ out of the pockets of the *players*, (-$) and puts it in the pockets of the Fat Cats."

Crazyman $ays: "The MASTERS are addicted to accumulating
                        wealth and power without remorse."

Crazyman $ays: "In pursuing something we want, our
                        emotions allow us to ignore the faults."

Crazyman $ays: "Don't believe what you think, are told, or
                        are taught. Follow your $, do your math,
                        facts are facts."

Fourth law
of motion: "For investors as a whole, returns decrease
                        as motion increases." – Warren Buffett

Crazyman $ays: "Professional advice doesn't guarantee good
                        advice."

Crazyman $ays: (investors > hedgers > speculators > traders
                        > clients = PLAYERS)

Crazyman $ays: "Published value and perceived value are the
                        greatest illusions of actual wealth."

Crazyman $ays: "The man who has $ in his pocket will eat
                        that night; the man who doesn't might go
                        hungry."

Crazyman $ays: "A main ingredient of the con game is
                        changing the value constantly."

Crazyman $ays: "If the losers' quit losing...the lights will go
                        out."

Crazyman $ays: "Our search for financial security is our
                        greatest vulnerability, and the Fat Cats'
                        greatest strength and opportunity."

Addendum Three:
— Terms for you to remember —

Masters of Illusion and Deception (MASTERS) – A group of highly influential, brilliant, and greedy people consisting of Wall Street leaders, government officials, corporate CEO's, brokers, and $ managers, who have used every available resource to build their empire by separating you from your money ($) without accountability or prosecution. The MASTERS developed and put the plan into motion.

Fat Cats – The select few (exchanges, high-level money managers, CEO's, government officials, etc.) who benefit from the plan of the MASTERS.

Players – This term replaces the terms investors, hedgers, traders, and speculators, and clients. By referring to *players*, I am always talking about them as a complete unit. These people put their money towards the purchase of shares in public-traded companies or commodity contracts. For the chapter on commodities, I would define a *player* as:
▶   a person with $ to risk,
▶   a person that doesn't have to have any qualifications to participate in the markets,
▶   a person buying and selling contracts on speculation,
▶   a person creating a price that the producers can use collectively and not be charged or prosecuted for price-fixing.

Eagle's Eye view – When I use the term "Eagle's Eye view," I'm emphasizing that you are misdirected to focus specifically on an individual or small picture view as opposed to looking at the complete overall picture. Remember to focus on *players* as a whole, not on an individual basis.

$ – I use the $ to emphasize that the whole purpose of the MASTERS is to separate you from your $, and replaces the word "money" throughout the remainder of the book.

Minus-sum game – This indicates that from the beginning, *players* as a whole have less $ in-pocket than they started with.

(-$) – This indicates that a *player* is losing $ as part of a transaction.

Zero-sum game – This is a neutral term used as a crutch by brokers that is an illusion either way. With fees and commissions on transactions, there is no possibility that the markets are ever a zero-sum game.

Investment – I've included this definition to emphasize why I don't use this word to describe what the markets offer. In a true investment, I'm referring to a transaction that has a 100 percent possibility of making $, and the $ you make will come from the profit of a product or a service. In the markets, it's impossible for 100 percent of the *players* to make $, and the $ they make comes primarily from other *players*.

Lost $ – The $ you have in pocket that is less than you started with.

Published value – A created illusion of wealth that cannot be counted as $ in pocket.

Perceived Value – A created illusion of wealth that conditions you to believe you have actual wealth without $ in pocket.

Outperformed – A created illusion of value that brokers use to make a poor or negative situation look positive. Without statistics, it has no true value.

"[Crazyman's Economics is] not a typical investment book, to be sure. Having read through it...I have to say that it is not crazy at all, but applies good, solid horse sense to the financial markets."
—Gary Weiss - Former *Business Week* senior writer and author of the acclaimed books, "Wall Street Versus America" and "Born to Stal."